Black Elk and
Flaming Rainbow

Hilda Neihardt

Black Elk and Flaming Rainbow

Personal Memories of the Lakota Holy Man and John Neihardt

University of Nebraska Press
Lincoln and London

The paper in this book
meets the minimum requirements
of American National Standard
for Information Sciences—
Permanence of Paper
for Printed Library Materials,
ANSI Z39.48-1984.

Library of Congress
Cataloging in
Publication Data

Petri, Hilda Neihardt.
Black Elk and Flaming Rainbow :
personal memories of the
Lakota holy man and
John Neihardt / Hilda Neihardt.
p. cm.
Includes index.
ISBN 0-8032-3338-8 (alk. paper)
1. Black Elk, 1863–1950.
2. Neihardt, John Gneisenau,
1881–1973.
3. Petri, Hilda Neihardt.
4. Oglala Indians—Biography.
5. Authors, American—
20th century–Biography.
I. Title.
E99.O3B5366   1995
978'.004975—dc20
[B]   94-26350   CIP
Second printing: 1995

Contents

Illustrations

Photographs from the John G. Neihardt Papers, Western Historical Manuscript Collection, Columbia, Missouri, are indicated by "Neihardt Papers" in the captions.

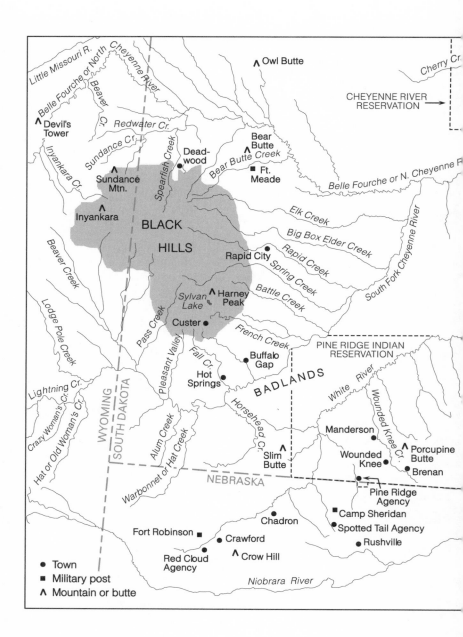

Preface

When I began to write this book, my intention was to tell the untold personal side of John Neihardt's interviews with Black Elk and Eagle Elk. My father, except in private conversations or public appearances, and perhaps also in the two autobiographical books written late in his life, did not emphasize the personal; he wrote always of the larger pattern. Because the experiences we had with the holy man Black Elk and his family and with the warrior Eagle Elk have remained important to me, and because my memory of those times is so vivid, it seemed worthwhile to record them. I do this now.

Throughout my story of the 1931 interviews, I cite dates when various events and discussions occurred. Those dates are correct, for they are taken from the diary kept at the time by my sister Enid Neihardt Fink, who acted as reporter for those interviews. I have quoted certain observations Enid made in that daily record, because her unstudied comments now recapture the simple freshness of the moment. It is also from Enid's diary that I was reminded that Neihardt had only three weeks on the Pine Ridge Reservation to complete the 1931 interviews, for she complains that such a limitation greatly increased the workload. I thank Enid most sincerely for granting me permission to make use of her 1931 diary in this story.

I do not intend to reiterate the content of the interviews, or to repeat what is available in *Black Elk Speaks* or *When the Tree Flowered*. There is, however, a substantial amount of material that is both interesting and of historical importance—stemming from the times of the interviews and from our association with the Black Elks and with

Eagle Elk—but that has not previously been recorded. In recounting such remembered material in this book, I have enriched my story and ensured the accuracy of my memory by turning to several sources. I have referred to the published transcripts of Enid's 1931 notes; I have myself transcribed from her shorthand tablets a number of letters my father dictated, as well as all of her diary; and I have checked my own typewritten reports made when I accompanied my father in 1944 to interview Black Elk and Eagle Elk.

For the most part, however, this book comes from my memory of the 1931 interviews, when I was a rather advanced high-school student; from my recollections of the summer of 1934 when my father, Alice, and I camped on Ben Black Elk's land while I was in college; and from the 1944 interviews when, in my twenty-eighth year, I acted as reporter for my father. What I tell here results likewise from my continued association with the subject matter throughout my life, enriched by my close rapport with my father during his lifetime.

During the several years taken to complete it, I have regarded the writing of this book as imperative because—except for Enid, who has been most helpful to me—no one else is still living who was present during the interviews. Black Elk himself, Eagle Elk, Ben, Ellen, Lucy, and Leo are all gone, and John Neihardt as well, which leaves to me the privilege of reporting this previously untold story.

It is not surprising, since *Black Elk Speaks* has attracted great interest both in this country and abroad, that the book has been the subject of varying interpretations, some of which reveal serious misunderstandings. Although portions of my story are devoted primarily to a human-interest narrative of what happened during our visits, other parts express certain critical facets of the Black Elk story. Among those facets I would include Black Elk's response to my father's question concerning the holy man's participation in a white church and what Lucy volunteered to me about the true religious beliefs of her father, her brother, and herself. I have related such facts and communications, which I consider essential to an understanding of the whole Black Elk story, simply and without embroidery, just as they unfolded naturally during talks with the holy man and with Ben and Lucy.

I wish for this, my telling, two things: I trust it will be clear to my readers that no part of my story, no incident in it, has been created or imagined by me. Quite as important is my heartfelt wish that this story will be an expression of the unforgettable warm, happy visits we had with those good people, the Black Elk family and their friends.

Black Elk and
Flaming Rainbow

The Wild Ones

"There they are! The wild ones!" Leo Looks Twice shouted. About a half mile away I saw them—some fifty or more spotted, bay, and black mustangs. And they saw us. The herd leader whinnied a command, and the horses bolted.

"Let's go!" Leo's bay gelding pushed off at a gallop, and I followed. Our horses stretched out in a dead run, and the strange South Dakota landscape opened before us in the cool early May morning—tall white bluffs, stunted pines, rough terrain partly covered with buffalo grass already begging for rain. The year 1931 was a dry one, and the normal spring rains stubbornly refused to come on Pine Ridge Reservation. The pounding hooves of the wild horses threw up clouds of dust, and we followed in little dust clouds of our own.

Many times, riding in the Missouri Ozarks with my sister Alice, I had felt the excitement of racing bareback, when the rider is carried almost motionless on the straining back, above those flying hooves. Those were happy times for both horse and rider, for horses love to run. But this was different; this was *more*. Feeling almost guilty in our wild abandon, I urged on my little buckskin mare, trying to keep up with Leo's big bay.

The high plateau gave way before us, and the wild horses suddenly disappeared from view. Without hesitation, Leo plunged down the steep hillside, somehow maneuvering his mount past boulders and over the rough ground. My little mare, true to the reputation of the dauntless buckskin, went right over the edge of the bluff-like hill without hesitation. I leaned back in the saddle; the mare settled on her haunches, and we skittered to the floor of the valley below. But our herd of mustangs had vanished: only pine trees, curly buffalo grass, and the wide, high, blue sky met our view.

More than once while we were with our Lakota friends on the reservation, Leo and I chased the "wild ones," but it was always the same: in that wide open country we were never able to get close enough to those four-leggeds for Leo to throw a rope, as I had often seen cowboys do in motion pictures. Instead we just watched them disappear in the distance.

Yes, those horses were wild—really wild, like deer—and Leo probably never expected to catch them on those expeditions. Now that I am no longer fourteen, I can see that it was the chase we loved, and that horses, man, and girl all rejoiced in their freedom to be wild.

On the way back to Black Elk's home, we chose a less precipitous route, and we let our horses take it easy at a slow lope. We even walked part of the way—Leo's concession to my query, "Won't it hurt the horses to run all the time?" "It won't hurt those horses none, Hilda." Leo chuckled at my concern. "Why, they won't have to do anything again for a month. We don't ride-out much anymore."

We topped a rise and reined in to look at the broad land below us. "Our place is right over there," Leo said, nodding to the east, "'bout three, four miles. We'll be back in plenty of time."

My little mare took a deep breath. Also relaxed, I did the same. I felt at home; I felt I belonged on those bluff-studded rough plains, dry and dusty under an empty sky that stretched around us in a great blue circle. And Leo Looks Twice, this husky young son-in-law of the Lakota holy man Black Elk, seemed like an older brother. I felt close to him, as I did to my real brother at home. In the naturalness of our friendship, I noticed our differences only as they intensified what I was experiencing. Brown Indian man and white Indian girl. No strangeness there!

As we rode toward Black Elk's home, Leo broke into a song. "It's kind of a love song," he answered my question. "Chiksuya waowe / Chante shica waowe / He o he! He o he!" (I remember you, *wa o we* / Heart bad [sad] *wa o we* / *He o he! He o he!*). As powerful, deep-chested Leo sang, the hills seemed to listen. I could not understand the language of the song, but I remember the sound of it. The melody was haunting, never to be forgotten. The strange, empty landscape, the Indian, the horses, and the beautiful song gave me a feeling of uplift I had never known before. Nor would I ever again, except in more than half a century of remembering, experience the joy, the wild abandon of that stretched-out moment.

It was hard to believe that this Lakota, this wild young Looks Twice who sang as we rode together, had almost frightened me when my father, my sister Enid, and I had arrived at Black Elk's log home a few days before.

Leo and I had been gone longer than we planned, and like tardy children who run as they near the schoolhouse, we came down the slope behind Black Elk's cabin at a gallop. When we arrived, everyone was inside eating a hearty breakfast. Hungry after our "ride-out," we hurriedly removed saddles and bridles, turned the horses loose, and washed some of the dust from our faces and hands. Fortunately Ellen and Lucy had saved us some eggs and potatoes on the back of the cookstove.

But I see I have gotten far ahead of myself, and we must go back almost a year, to August 1930, when this story began.

Back Home
in Branson

Our home in the Missouri Ozarks was a two-story stuccoed farm-house on the edge of Branson. Today the bustling center of a thriving tourist industry, in 1930 Branson was a sleepy little town of about a thousand people, many of them retirees who had come to enjoy the beauty of the Ozark Mountains. The area had much to offer those who lived there and those who came to vacation on Lake Taneycomo. All felt the charm of the beautiful hill country as they drove along crude roads or rode horseback over mountain trails. Our local taxi driver, Pearl Spurlock, told how tourists, captivated by the views of blue, haze-covered mountains, had accidents when they drove off the nar-row, curving roads.

Our family included my parents, Grandma Neihardt, my older sis-ter Enid, my older brother, Sigurd, my younger sister Alice, and me. We had moved in 1920 from Bancroft in the farmlands of northeastern Nebraska, where my father's early works had been written and where my parents had lived for twelve years after their marriage. Lovers of the outdoors, my mother and father were lured by the Ozark moun-tain country, then quite unspoiled, and the promise of winters less harsh than in Nebraska.

But there was more to it than the weather, for my mother, Mona Martinsen Neihardt, said the Ozarks reminded her of the Black Forest in southern Germany, where she had spent many happy years as a child at her family's summer home. Pictures of that home hung in the Bran-son house, and the Martinsen home, called Vromberg, looked like a castle to us. The Martinsens were wealthy, and Grandfather Martinsen was an international financier—a banker in Amsterdam with Boissevain et Cie and also president of several American firms, among them the Missouri, Kansas, and Texas Railroad, the Northern Pacific Railroad, and the Consolidated Coal Company in Wyoming.

Mona Martinsen had grown up in Europe and New York: in Europe because that was their home base, and in New York because Rudolf Martinsen believed deeply in the future of the United States and wanted all his children to be American born. I recall our mother's telling about the many trips between Europe and America the family had made by sailing vessel when she was a girl—fourteen, I think. While in New York on business, Grandfather Martinsen was stricken by a heart attack when only forty years of age, and the family hurried to his side. Traveling by boat was slow, and they arrived in New York too late. Mother, who was particularly attached to her father, never entirely recovered from his premature death.

The family continued to live in Germany for some time, but after a few years the beloved Black Forest home was sold, and Mother's mother, Adah Ernst Martinsen, originally from Richmond, Indiana, took her children to live in New York. It was there that Mona's artistic ability revealed itself when she created a portrait bust of one of her brothers from bread dough the cook was preparing. Adah Martinsen, greatly impressed, showed this little bust to Frank Elwell, curator of the New York Museum of Art. He too recognized Mona's latent ability, agreed to consider taking her as a pupil, and set a time for her to come to his studio.

When the excited young woman reported to Elwell's studio, he showed her an equestrian statue he was working on, pointed out the rider's unfinished boot, and told her to complete it for him. Then he left for lunch. When he returned he inspected what Mona had done, approved, and agreed to take her as his pupil.

After he had worked with her for some time, Elwell told her mother that Mona showed such promise that he felt she would benefit from study with someone more advanced than he was. The great Auguste Rodin was suggested. Adah Martinsen found a friend who would contribute to the expense of study with the famous sculptor, and Mona was sent to Paris. Mother told us how she first met Rodin. She was crossing a street near his studio when she saw him coming. She hurried toward him and called out, "Monsieur Rodin!" When he stopped and turned, she told him she had come all the way from New York to study with him. Removing his hat and bowing, Rodin replied, "Enchanté, mademoiselle!" It was all set: Mona Martinsen would study with Auguste Rodin!

In 1907 a little book containing John Neihardt's early lyrics, many of them passionate and, for the times, "frank" love poems, had been published under the title *A Bundle of Myrrh*. Successful in New York, the book made its way to Paris, and copies were being passed around among students in the artists' colony there. Mona Martinsen read the poems and was captivated. She wrote to the young midwestern poet, breathing these words as she posted the letter: "Dear God! Let him not be married!"

Fortunately the young Nebraska poet *wasn't* married, though the enthusiastic reception of his poetry in New York and elsewhere had created a following, and he had received letters from many appreciative young ladies. He told us later, "Yes, I got many letters, but hers were the best."

Neihardt answered Mona's letter, and a correspondence followed between Paris and Bancroft that would, I am sure, have made quite a love story in itself had the letters not been destroyed in a fire. I remember how my brother used to sneak those letters out of their box in the attic, read them, and giggle. I could not yet read at that time, so I can only guess what they said. No doubt the two gave each other considerable personal information, and they exchanged photographs. One thing is certain: the letters contained a proposal of marriage and an acceptance.

And so it was that on November 28, 1908, a tall, well-dressed, obviously cosmopolitan young woman, her long hair carefully coiffed "up" and wearing a broad-brimmed velvet hat, alighted gracefully from the train at Union Station in Omaha, Nebraska. There to meet her, in a fine new suit and with a marriage license in his hip pocket, was John Neihardt. "Then it was that I saw her for the first time with my eyes," he told us later, confiding that his first impulse was to turn and run! She was so different, so stylish, so *tall*. Yes, each knew the other's height, but she stood *inches* above him, and no doubt he must have worried about what she would think when she actually saw him. But she called out eagerly, "John! John!" Her warm greeting made everything all right, and he hurried to meet her.

They were married the next day at the home of Keene Abbot, a friend on the Omaha *Bee,* then took the train to Bancroft, where they would live.

One might fear that a marriage so romantically conceived and between people from such disparate backgrounds could not succeed. But they believed fervently in the same higher values, the most important basis for a life together. Fifty years later we children were planning a celebration for their golden wedding anniversary when our mother died from a minor automobile accident. Daddy expressed his desperate loss: "She had built herself into the walls of my world."

If I have seemed to stray from telling about our life in the Ozarks, it is because this story would be incomplete without describing how John and Mona Neihardt came together. For after their marriage in 1908 any discussion of John Neihardt would be incomplete without something about the woman he lovingly called "my Mona"—and not just incomplete, but inaccurate.

To me our life seemed idyllic. In the summers we children went barefoot from May to September; we swam in the crystal waters of Roark Creek, and we fished and boated with our father on the White River, then dammed to form Lake Taneycomo. The big dam that created Tablerock Lake and spawned the present frantic commercialism was then only a vague dream of certain promoters and a distant hope that residents expressed from time to time.

As "furriners" in the Ozarks, we had quickly learned that in summertime it was best to avoid the forests, where troublesome wood ticks abounded. After the first freeze in the fall, however, we hiked those rugged and rocky hills and camped out in the primitive, self-sufficient way my father loved. We all enjoyed the challenge of finding food and water and keeping warm on a winter's night with little equipment. My sister Alice, born a year after we arrived in Branson, and I never missed a chance to go on such impromptu camping trips. It was great fun to do things with our dad.

My father's personality combined in a most intriguing way the talents of the artist with those of an intensely practical man—he could fix or make almost anything. He often said that before one professed to be an artist, one should live up to one's responsibilities as a person. He felt that one becomes truly educated only by becoming aware, as he put it, of the "best that people have thought and felt and done throughout history." This awareness was to be arrived at through great literature.

So it was that on our camping, hiking, or horseback expeditions, poetry was never left behind. I recall, and so does Alice, his clear, melodious voice reciting from Virgil's *Aeneid,* from Tennyson, or Swinburne—or Neihardt—as we hurried to keep up with him on foot through the winter woods, as we sat around a campfire at night, or as one of us clung to the saddle behind him as he urged his mare, Ribbon, to do her best on the rocky roads. Ribbon had been a harness pacer, and she was so fast that other horses had to gallop to keep up.

Later we had a Kentucky saddle mare, black as coal, who surely deserved the fond name we gave her—Pet. Pet was our own horse, but Ribbon belonged to a local stable catering to tourists, and her owner was glad to have us keep a horse or two over the winter. He knew that with us his horses would eat well, relieving him of the cost of their upkeep, and that they would be in good shape and—especially—more manageable when returned to him in the spring. Alice and I were good with horses.

In the summer of 1930 we were at home in the Missouri Ozarks, eagerly awaiting the return of my father and my brother Sigurd from a lecture tour to colleges in the Midwest, which they had combined with a special trip to the Pine Ridge Indian Reservation in southwestern South Dakota. In those days part of our dad's income was from book royalties, but the main support for the family came from his lecturing at colleges and universities and from literary criticism done for various newspapers. My father was working on *The Song of the Messiah* at the time. Most of the research and planning for the book were done, and he had already written the first five hundred lines, but he wanted to find and get close to a Sioux holy man who had participated in the Ghost Dance movement, which spread through many western Indian tribes during the 1880s.

As many know, the American Indian people first welcomed, then resisted the westward-pushing whites, who seemed to come in great waves—always more, endlessly more. It seemed that the Indians' good way of life might soon be gone forever. The whites' diseases had cut a swath of suffering and death through various tribes, and many were faced with starvation. The deer and buffalo, which the Plains tribes depended on for food, shelter, and clothing, were being senselessly slaughtered by hunters—first for profit, then for the mere sport of killing. The land they lived on was being taken, and the wide plains of Mother Earth, which they believed to be a living being, were repeatedly violated by the settlers' plows and cut up by fences, roads, and railroad tracks.

It was all strange and wrong to the invaded ones, but they could not stop the oncoming flood of whites, however bravely they fought against it. And so, as people do when faced with seemingly insurmountable difficulty, they turned to dreams and the hope of spiritual intervention. Thus it was about 1889 that the Ghost Dance movement was born. The news came that out west in Nevada a Paiute named Wovoka had had a strange dream in which it seemed that he died and went to the spirit world, where he was told what the Indian people must do to survive. They must pray, they must paint themselves in the sacred manner he was shown in his vision, and they must dance a certain dance he would teach them. If they did all this, the whites would disappear, buffalo and dead Indians would come back, and the dear earth would be renewed. People and plants and animals would live happily forever on a green, green earth, under a blue, blue sky. And so they danced in the day, in the night, in the snow, and they wore Ghost Dance shirts made of flour sacks and painted themselves in the sacred manner Wovoka had been taught in his vision. Some dancers fell trance-like to the ground and had visions of their own.

Because most white people did not understand the meaning of all that dancing, which seemed foolish to them, it was called the "Ghost Dance craze." Thinking the nearly destitute, unarmed Indians were preparing for war, they called on the army for protection—*protection from dancing!*

As history records, this vision-inspired hope of the Plains tribes ended tragically in the bloody snow of the Wounded Knee massacre on December 29, 1890. This happening would mark the end of organized Indian resistance on the plains, and it would also be the end of my father's *Cycle of the West.*

Neihardt gave life to his writings by combining historical research with firsthand accounts from persons who had participated in the great drama of our western history. In the early part of the twentieth century this was still possible, for many old-timers—settlers, soldiers, and Indians, both men and women—were still living. My father sought them out. "I made it my business," he told us, "to find people who had *lived* our history and talk to them. That way I could get a real feel for the times—make them *come alive.*" Such was the purpose of the trip from which Daddy and Sigurd would soon return.

It was always exciting for us when our dad came home from a lecture tour; this time it was particularly so. On our daily trip by horseback to town for the mail, Alice and I found a letter from Daddy. I'm sure we got home faster than usual that day to hear what the letter might say. We tied Pet to the big maple tree near the back door and ran breathless to our mother, who opened the envelope eagerly.

"Daddy and Sigurd will be coming back soon—probably in a day or two," Mama announced, adding that Daddy had some "great news" to tell us when he arrived. "Let's get everything neat and ready before they get here," Mama said. "We want the house to look beautiful when Daddy arrives."

So we all helped a bit. Our mother, who had continued with her art after her marriage, had more time to work on her sculpture when Daddy was away, and we understood that household duties sometimes had to give way. I loved this tall, glowing woman, our mother. Although she did not complain about the life she had chosen, even as a child I sensed that life was not entirely fair to her. In those days housekeeping was endless, back-breaking work that did not seem appropriate for someone so refined, so artistic.

While we were all scurrying about helping Mother with our cleanup duties, a telephone call came from Western Union, and a wire from Daddy was read that probably ran something like this: "Arriving home tomorrow. Stop. Have wonderful news. Stop. Love, John."

Daddy and Sigurd did arrive the next day, about noon. We all ran out to the car, my mother calling out in her enthusiastic way, "Oh, John! I'm so glad you're home!" We gathered around the returning pair, and I stood quietly by, waiting for a greeting. Then my dad turned to me, smiling and patting my cheek as he had done when I was small. "And how are you, Hiddy?"

They were home! And now for that bit of good news!

But first there was dinner, which Mother, with Enid's help, had prepared on the woodstove. While we ate, Daddy and Sigurd told us about their trip. I shall try to recall here only the momentous news— the story of their meeting with Black Elk.

An Accidental
Meeting

Much like the cracker-barrel crowd at an old-time general store, a group of old Sioux men were gathered at the red-brick agency office in Pine Ridge, catching up on the local news. I can imagine their politely curious glances as the smallish, middle-aged man and his tall young son parked a Missouri-licensed car and strode into the agency building.

Agent Courtwright was in, and they exchanged friendly greetings. After a bit my father explained the reason for the visit and inquired whether the agent knew of a Lakota holy man who had been active in the 1880s and had taken part in the "Ghost Dance craze." The agent searched his memory but could think of no such person; then he put the question to the assembled Sioux. The old men talked among themselves in Lakota for a time; then one spoke, and someone relayed in English what he said.

They told of an old man who lived in the hills west of Manderson: Black Elk, they said, had taken part in the Ghost Dance movement and was "kind of a preacher," but he might not be willing to talk. Undaunted, my father asked if someone there would go with him and act as interpreter, since he was told Black Elk did not speak English.

The trip was soon arranged. A Lakota named Flying Hawk, who spoke English fairly well, agreed to show my father and Sigurd the way to Black Elk's home. The three left immediately and drove from Pine Ridge to Manderson, and then to the one-room log house a few miles west of town where the old "preacher" lived. On the way, Flying Hawk told my father he had recently taken a woman from Lincoln,

Nebraska, to see Black Elk, a writer who wanted to interview the old Sioux. But, he said, Black Elk had refused to talk to her. My father responded that he had known Indians for many years, and they had always talked to him.

The narrow road from Manderson was deep with dust, which mounted in a cloud as they drove. Near the top of a low, bare hill stood an old log cabin. Quite alone in a pine shelter near the house was a slender, oldish Indian. He wore a wrinkled and well-worn white man's suit, and his gray hair was cut short. He shaded his eyes as he peered down the road at the automobile coming up the hill to his home.

"How, kola," Flying Hawk said as they got out of the car, and Black Elk returned his greeting in Lakota. Then Flying Hawk introduced the two Neihardts. Black Elk acknowledged them courteously, but with the quiet reserve we would later come to know.

My father had brought cigarettes and other small gifts, which the old man received with dignified appreciation. It was apparent that Black Elk was nearly blind, and he squinted in an effort to see his guests. After some introductory chatting, not wishing to appear discourteously hasty, Neihardt explained why he had come. Modestly, he gave enough background about his writings and his thirty years' acquaintance with people of the Omaha and Sioux tribes to lend credence to his quest.

He said he had come to meet Black Elk because he had learned he was a *wichasha wakan*—a holy man—and had taken part in the Ghost Dance movement. Explaining his interest, Neihardt told the old holy man he had just completed a book of poetry about the struggles between the Indians and the whites who were taking his people's homeland. That book, *The Song of the Indian Wars,* ended, he said, with the death of the great Sioux leader Crazy Horse.

Black Elk had been listening politely as Flying Hawk translated what Neihardt was saying, but at this point he interrupted to state that Crazy Horse—Tashunka Witco—was his second cousin. My father acknowledged this important fact, then said that a Major Lemly, who was stationed at Fort Robinson when Crazy Horse was killed there, had told him what happened on that day. Major Lemly was so angry, my father related, about the way Black Elk's great cousin and his parents were treated that he asked to be transferred out of the Indian Service. Then, after a pause, my father added that there were good men on both sides of the struggle.

Black Elk agreed: "Hmmm." Then he fell into a thoughtful silence.

For a time my father asked questions that he thought might encourage Black Elk to talk about the ghost dancing or to share any other memories of his life during that period. It became evident that Black Elk was not particularly interested in historical matters: to each question my father posed, he responded politely but briefly. Clearly he was preoccupied with something more meaningful to him. Several times he mentioned a vision he had had when he was nine years old, and each time an air of deep sorrow seemed to envelop the old Lakota.

Then, more silence. My father understood and asked no more questions. The men smoked quietly together.

After some minutes, Black Elk began to speak, directing what he said more toward the ground or the empty landscape in front of him than to his visitors. What Black Elk said then was momentous, and I have heard my father tell it so many times that I feel I could quote him verbatim. Having watched Black Elk during many days, I can also visualize that first meeting.

Turning to the interpreter, Black Elk said that he felt in the man beside him a great desire to know the things of the other world, and that he believed this man he had so newly met "had been sent" to save what he would tell him. Referring to his vision, he remarked that if it was great and mighty when it was given to him, it was still great and mighty, and that it was for all people. Black Elk announced that soon he himself would be under the grass, but that the man sitting by him in the pine shade was to save the vision for all people.

Then he said that Neihardt must return in the spring to learn what Black Elk would teach him. Neihardt was deeply impressed but, sensing that Black Elk was not finished, made no response, waiting for the holy man to continue.

During this conversation, several members of Black Elk's family had come out of the cabin, one by one, and gathered nearby, respectfully silent. Also, a number of neighbors who had noticed the arrival of an automobile had come on horseback and were politely sitting partway down the hill so they would be the first to know whatever news might be forthcoming.

Now Black Elk spoke to a young boy, perhaps a grandson, waving his hand toward the cabin. The boy went inside and returned with a simple necklace made of rawhide thongs already stiff with age. Black Elk took the necklace, held it before him, and explained its significance.

Showing a circular piece of rawhide decorated with a painted design with small triangular indentations cut around its circumference, he described it as the daybreak star. Who sees the daybreak star, he said, shall have wisdom, and from that wisdom the peace that comes only from understanding. Then he pointed out a piece of fur on the thong, which he said represented Mother Earth and all the good things of this life: food, clothing, and a place to live. Reverently he touched a feather that also hung from the thong. What he said about the feather was inspiring to my father then and has been so to me all my life. That eagle feather, he commented, meant that our thoughts should rise high as the eagle does.

Turning to his visitor, Black Elk offered him the necklace, saying he wished for his friend all the good things the necklace represented. He gave the necklace to my father!

Deeply impressed, the poet Neihardt thanked the holy man for the gift, assuring him that he would cherish it and keep it with him always.

Then he eagerly asked when Black Elk wanted him to come back, saying that he would spend time with the holy man and learn what he would teach him. Black Elk responded that he must return in the spring when the grass was "so high"—the width of his hand. Earnestly Neihardt promised to come back then and listen to what Black Elk would tell him, and to put what he learned into a true and beautiful book. As the holy man wished, that book would save his teachings and tell his great vision for all people.

Black Elk nodded his approval.

My father and brother then bade a fond farewell to the holy man and his family. The words "fond farewell" are used truly, for the afternoon had been a very special one, and both men felt a warm affection for the old Indian. But more than that, John Neihardt was moved as he had seldom been. Black Elk's fleeting references to his vision were, Daddy told us later, "like flashes of sheet lightning on a summer night that reveal a strange and beautiful landscape."

As the three men drove back to the agency office, Flying Hawk commented in a mystified way that it seemed the old man had been *waiting* for Neihardt. My brother responded that he too had noticed Black Elk seemed to be expecting them. It appeared, he said, that the old man was looking down the road as they drove up, and he did not seem a bit surprised by their arrival. But, Sigurd insisted, there was no way Black Elk could possibly have learned he would have visitors. In 1930 there were few telephones or automobiles on the reservation, and certainly there had not been time for anyone on horseback to ride to Black Elk's home and tell him.

Flying Hawk merely shook his head, describing him as a "funny old man." Black Elk had simpler ways of knowing.

A Book Is
Conceived

The ripples from Dad's and Sigurd's excitement about their "chance" meeting with Black Elk quickly spread through the Neihardt family. To me their story had the air of an Arabian Nights tale, for they had ventured into a world I had only read about.

It is probable that on the very day of his return Daddy went to town and sent a wire to a New York publisher he knew personally—William Morrow—briefly describing his trip and Black Elk and asking if Morrow was interested in hearing more. He was, and Dad wrote a letter about the trip and the remarkable man he had met. Since his return, his thoughts had been on Black Elk and what he wanted to tell, and also on what he anticipated the old man's life experiences would reveal. He became convinced that the proposed book should give not only the story of the holy man's life but also the story of his people during the period—that it should go beyond a description of the great vision.

Hearing what Black Elk revealed in their first meeting must have been to my writer father much like a hiker's suddenly coming upon an opening in the mountains, to see stretched before him a land of unparalleled beauty he had unconsciously been seeking. He sensed that something new would come from interviews, and he wrote to both William Morrow and Black Elk about what he thought the scope of the book should be.

To Morrow he pointed out that this old holy man had lived the old-time nomadic life of the Plains Indians. Not only had he been given a vision that promised to be of rare beauty, he had also been a hunter and a warrior. The story of his life, my father urged, would make a book "unlike any that had yet been written—a book truly *Indian* from the inside out." He added that Black Elk had several friends whose experiences would enrich the old man's story.

To Black Elk he wrote that his life story, together with what his old friends could contribute, would make a beautiful book. "It will be the story of your people," Neihardt told him, "and it will be honest and true."

The publisher and the Lakota holy man were both interested. Morrow agreed to publish the book and to give an advance on royalties of one thousand dollars, an amount that was adequate for those times but now would seem laughable. The advance, well managed, would make it possible to go to Pine Ridge Reservation, spend time with Black Elk and his family, and conduct interviews with the holy man and his friends.

Big plans were made during the following fall and winter. Alice and I changed from jeans to dresses, put on shoes, and went back to classes, where I was in my second year of high school. Enid had finished high school and had chosen to attend a business college in St. Louis. Sigurd, who aspired to become a concert pianist, would go to St. Louis to continue his musical training and study auto mechanics. What a combination!

Except when he was employed by a newspaper, our father worked at home, where a book-lined room was set aside for his writing. He reported to his study faithfully each morning after breakfast, and Mother made it clear that he must not be disturbed. It was his custom to come out, perhaps during the morning, perhaps not until the noon dinner, and read to Mother the lines he had been able to "get" on that day. Mama's face was radiant as she listened, and her enthusiastic responses must have given him the support he needed: "Oh, John, that's great stuff!"

Other members of the family—whoever happened to be present—listened as well. I can still relive the setting and remember in a dream-like way my feelings when he read for the first time certain lines from his *Cycle of the West*. Our lives revolved around Daddy and his writings; from the very air we absorbed a pervasive devotion to what Mother called "his great work."

Both being artists, my parents had much to talk about, and they found quiet time to do so over coffee at early breakfast. Because I wanted to be part of these mysterious early mornings, I earned the nickname "our little early riser." Perhaps some will remember a patent medicine that claimed to have such an effect.

Since I was quite young, I had loved to get up in the "chilly dark" and slip ever so quietly down the stairs to the dining room, there to sit in the loving warmth of my father and mother. And listen. Their conversations remain in my memory as a tapestry woven of the ideas they shared, whose meanings I could then hardly comprehend. I do remember many of their recurring words. They spoke of art, poetry, the beauty and sorrows of life, and—above all—their unswerving belief that the pursuit of what they called "the higher values" was worth all the desperate effort it might demand. I particularly remember those magical words "the higher values," for they were used often. It seemed clear to me that whatever those words meant must be wonderful indeed!

That winter they talked much about Black Elk. My father's letters to him were answered by his son Ben, his daughter, Lucy, or perhaps at times by Ben's wife, Ellen. Gradually plans were made for the trip and for the interviews. At my father's request, Black Elk invited several of his friends to participate in the talks. He stipulated that his son Ben should act as interpreter. Ben had gone to school away from the reservation and knew English fairly well, but he was chosen for other important reasons: Black Elk planned to talk about sacred matters, and what he would tell should be heard only by one very near to him. Also, he wanted to be sure that his interpreter honestly translated what he said, and he trusted Ben. Standing Bear, his oldest and best friend, would also be present at all times, to attest that Black Elk was telling the truth.

Neihardt agreed. Further, he assured Black Elk that he, Ben, and the other storytellers would be compensated for the time they spent in the interviews at a daily rate to be determined as fair. "I will pay you well," Neihardt wrote. Black Elk seemed pleased with the arrangements, and he invited my father and his daughters, who would accompany him, to stay with his family at the cabin near Manderson.

There! I've said it: "his *daughters*." My parents had decided that Enid, who was proficient in Gregg shorthand, would record the conversations, and that I might go along as what my dad humorously designated the "official observer." Enid, a very pretty and, in my eyes, grown-up young woman of nineteen, had already tested her skills in a business job.

As for me, well, I was much less mature and perhaps a strange combination, but I was ready to tackle my job. I loved the outdoors and the exhilarating sense of freedom one could experience away from household duties, which I did not enjoy, but I was also an avid reader. Daddy directed my reading program, and the school principal had given me permission to read during study halls. We children had received considerable instruction at home, and my high-school studies did not present much challenge. At this particular time I was engrossed in Homer's *Iliad* and *Odyssey,* and my vicarious participation in the wanderings of the Greek heroes enriched our own outdoor adventures. Or have I perhaps said that backward?

I do not doubt that the type of child I was may have entered into my parents' decision to include me in the great trip. Equally motivating, I suspect, was the thought that it would make things more pleasant for Enid, even if she was quite grown-up, to have another member of the family along. Since Alice was not yet ten, she was a bit young. Sigurd was too busy with his own affairs. And Mama—well, she was the anchor for our home, and in her warm and loving way she was always eager for us children "to do things with Daddy." Although I did not realize it then, the interludes when some of us were away camping, hiking, or in this instance traveling must have provided a welcome relief for our mother. Whether planned this way or not, those absences undoubtedly made it easier for her to find time for the art she loved.

But enough of such introspective background. Plans were being made for our departure the next spring, and since school would still be in session when we intended to leave, it was necessary to obtain permission for me to leave about a month before its closing. Being a thoroughly normal child, I hardly found this a tragedy.

I well remember the earnest face of Taylor McMaster, the handsome, dark-haired young Branson High School principal, as he told me I would be excused. For some reason his words impressed me and have remained with me these many years: "Yes, you may be excused to go with your father. The experience will be more valuable to you than the school time you will miss, Hilda." I also remember my feelings: it seemed so obvious that the trip would be more valuable that saying so was unnecessary. But he was a very nice man, and I did thank him for his kindness. I still keep in contact with his widow, Annabelle Kerr McMaster, who was also my teacher when I was in high school and who now lives not far from Branson.

As was customary on most of my dad's trips, this one would include several stops for lectures. The visits to colleges and his recitations of his lyric poetry and of excerpts from his *Cycle of the West,* then only partly completed, would be a new experience for Enid and me. Their primary purpose, of course, was the income they would produce.

After months of waiting, the day finally came. Early on May 1, 1931, Daddy, Enid, and I left Branson and took the gravel highway north through Springfield, Missouri—good old Missouri 55. Our 1929 Gardner was packed with our clothing and camping gear, and the three of us were a bit crowded in the narrow front seat. But never mind that; we were on our way!

And what were our feelings as we set out on our great adventure? It was the long-awaited moment, and our excitement, I feel sure, differed not much from the feelings of history's better-known adventurers. As Daddy would later express the spirit of adventure in his *Song of Jed Smith:*

There was a place to go to and we went,
High-hearted with a hunger for the New.

We Travel to
Black Elk's Home

Highways in the thirties were narrow and mostly unpaved, and a day of travel seemed long. The roar of the engine and the sound of the tires on rough roads were monotonous, and travelers arrived at their destinations dusty and weary.

That first night we stopped at a cabin camp in Holden, Kansas. Much different from today's motels, the cabin camp was just that—a group of separate cabins with primitive indoor or sometimes outdoor plumbing. They often had kitchens, which might contain cooking utensils and dishes, but sheets, towels, and other necessities were carried by the travelers. We cooked meals and made up beds before retiring, and there were no television sets or radios. But we were accustomed to providing our own entertainment, and we were happy. There were card games to play, and conversations with our dad were inventive and always fun.

The next morning we washed dishes, stripped the beds, packed our belongings in the Gardner, and took to the road about eight o'clock, according to Enid's diary, arriving at 2133 South 22d Street in Lincoln, the home of my father's Uncle Charles and Aunt Martha Culler, about three in the afternoon. My great-aunt and great-uncle greeted us warmly, and Aunt Martha promptly showed us to rooms upstairs in the comfortable house. Daddy was to speak at a banquet in the Hotel Lincoln that evening, and a bath and change of clothes soon made us feel ready for the exciting event. Enid and I did not often have an opportunity to hear our father speak to an audience.

I remember that Aunt Martha and Uncle Charles thought we

looked very pretty in the new dresses Mother had made for the occasion. We both felt very dressed up and a trifle stiff in our new clothes. I don't remember what our dresses looked like, but I did think Aunt Martha's dress was both beautiful and unusual. When I told her so Aunt Martha responded laughing, "Oh, Hilda, this is only a $16.95 dress!" I remember thinking, "Sixteen dollars and ninety-five cents? No *wonder* it's so beautiful." But that was a good many years ago, and times have changed.

It was great fun visiting them. My great-uncle, the principal of a Lincoln junior high school, was a warm, rich-spirited man, and he teased us in a most endearing way. It was easy to feel close to Uncle Charles, but I admired peppery and precise Aunt Martha from afar. Her neat, well-ordered home was evidence, as she clearly believed, that she did everything just as it should be done. I felt that her strong ideas went far beyond mere housekeeping (for which I then had little respect), and somehow this "just rightness" was both comforting and disconcerting to a fourteen-year-old who dreamed of larger freedoms. Perhaps the neighbors back home in Branson were right: maybe I was what was then called a tomboy.

To Enid and me, the evening at Hotel Lincoln was a brilliant affair. Enid's diary recorded, "I had so many handshakes that I was loose in the wrist. Daddy read beautifully." As for me, I was in high spirits and I blush to recall something that happened during the reception that followed the lecture. We were all proceeding up a broad stairway, and I walked behind a tall, dignified lady whose satin dress featured a floor-length sash. The temptation was too great: my days of "playing horse" were not far enough removed, and I took hold of the ends of her sash and "drove" her partway up the stairway. Although she was coolly gracious toward the daughter of the man of the hour, I realize now, if I did not then, that she did not share my enjoyment of that foolish prank.

The big evening was soon over, and Uncle Charles came for us in his Essex. Back at the Culler home Aunt Martha sent us girls upstairs to bed, but the three grown-ups chatted for a while in the kitchen over coffee and something good to eat. Like most performers, our father found it difficult to relax after one of his "stunts," as he called them.

The next day we drove to Omaha, about fifty miles from Lincoln, where we were expected at the home of Leigh Leslie, a longtime friend of our father's. The evening proved to be special, though downright frightening to me, for Mr. Leslie had arranged for his two nephews to take Enid and me to dinner and a movie. I recall feeling both uncomfortable and excited during the evening, but the young men and Enid seemed quite at ease and greatly enjoyed the meal. Eating out was a novelty I easily took in stride; eating out with *boys* was quite another thing! However, I was rescued by the movie, which Enid's diary identifies as the now infamous *Birth of a Nation*.

Back at the Leslie house, more entertainment awaited us: we listened to the radio! We didn't yet have one in our Branson home, but Grandma Neihardt, right next door, had an Atwater Kent radio with a separate hornlike speaker. Although it was not our first experience with that scientific marvel, listening to the radio was still important enough to be included in Enid's diary.

On May 4 we left Omaha at about eleven in the morning and took Highway 73 bound for Wayne, Nebraska, for another lecture appearance. On the way we stopped at Fort Calhoun and saw the old fort, which interested our history-minded father more than it did us. Like most teenagers, we were eager to reach our destination. On the way we stopped in Bancroft to see our old home, where both Enid and I had been born. In her diary Enid comments, "My, it's different! The house is the same, but the trees and shrubs are all much larger than before." Having been so young when the family left Bancroft for Missouri, I didn't remember anything about the place.

It was while living in Bancroft, on the edge of the Omaha Indian reservation, that my father had first come to know Indian people. He worked for an Indian trader, J. J. Elkin, and in the course of his job he came in contact with the Omahas and grew to respect them for their kindness to him and their spirituality. "He is a good young man," they had said; "he has the heart of an Indian." Because of his small stature but powerful build, the Omahas named him Tae Nuga Zhinga, Little Bull Buffalo. Neihardt was welcomed into their homes, and he visited often, eating with them and staying late into the night to hear the stories of their people as they were dramatically related by first one storyteller and then another. Rather than considering them hostile savages, as Indians were commonly seen in the early years of the twentieth century, or curiosities, as they are often sentimentally viewed, he saw the Omahas simply as good *people,* and his many short stories revealed their spirituality and much of their culture. His first literary success came with these stories.

Apparently we spent quite a bit of time looking around Bancroft, for Enid's diary reports that we arrived in Wayne, only some forty miles northwest, shortly before eight in the evening. We had been invited to stay at the home of President and Mrs. Conn on the Wayne State Normal campus. It was a Victorian two-story residence, and I thought it fine indeed. President Conn, a tall, gray-haired gentleman who had been my father's Latin professor many years before, greeted us in the dignified manner I would later come to know when I attended Wayne State. Mrs. Conn was witty and warm and had a particular talent for making strangers feel at home.

We spent two days at the school, which was of memorable importance to my father. He had graduated from the scientific course there in 1897, when he was sixteen. Because his studies had opened up a new world of possibilities, he later referred to the college as his "hill of vision."

It was this strong attachment that prompted him later to suggest that I attend there, and I did so for two of my happiest college years. While we were in Wayne, Daddy recited from his works at chapel, after which, Enid reports in her diary, "The crowd applauded freely as usual."

The next day, May 7, we visited with the Conns, then loaded our car before a noon dinner. Rather sadly we said good-bye to these good people, and an easy afternoon's drive brought us to a cabin camp in Long Pine, Nebraska, a small town on Highway 20 a little more than halfway across the state. It was an unusually pretty camp. Enid and I found a boat on a nearby waterway and had a fine time rowing around until our dad called us in for supper. He had done the cooking by himself this time, though usually Enid helped.

A few games of seven-up or casino and we went to bed, to sleep well in the fresh air. In those safe times windows could be left open at night, and one was not at the mercy of air conditioning. When we awoke we found that something had happened during the night that we would seldom see on our trip. It had rained. Normally this would not be worth noting, but the summer of 1931 would prove very dry.

The road was muddy that morning, and in Nebraska that is something to cope with, for when the deep soil is wet it gets very slick, almost greasy. We started out, got badly stuck, and were helped, Enid tells us, by a cheerful, breezy westerner in a Chevy. We returned to Long Pine, bought chains for the car, then set out once more on our way west. But it was a bad day for driving, and we repeatedly ran into trouble on the wet roads. I remember that once Daddy and I took off our outer clothes, got out, and pushed the Gardner while Enid drove. Returning to the car, we at least had some dry things to put on. Our Dad always had a plan.

In spite of the roads, we did make it to Valentine, Nebraska, where the rain had stopped. We put in at a cabin camp, where we cleaned up from our muddy adventure and donned fresh clothes. What a treat! On this trip Enid and I wore pants, which most certainly was not usual for women and girls in 1931. Even in our tourist town in the Ozarks, girls wore dresses. Back home, Enid wore slacks or jeans when she rode horseback, and I wore them instead of dresses most of the time. When we hiked through brush-filled forests, Daddy disliked having loose trousers catch on briars and branches, so we wore breeches and boots or leggings. On this trip all three of us wore tight-legged jodhpurs or breeches and lace-up boots that came to just below the knee. Leather boots also were a precaution in areas where rattlesnakes might be found. I recall no encounters with snakes, however. We never left clothes or bedding on the ground in tent or teepee during the daytime, and we carefully inspected the floor of our tent before retiring at night. So no snake problems.

But back to our trip. Valentine, on the Niobrara River in western Nebraska, was a very "western" town in those days. A rustic rodeo arena we passed reminded me of my beloved Will James stories. As I looked at the arena, I could see in my mind's eye the bucking horses and the cowboys "fanning" with their hats and raking their spurs over the broncs' shoulders, urging them to ever more frantic efforts to un-

Agency office in Pine Ridge, South Dakota, 1936. It was old men like those in the picture who told Neihardt about Black Elk in August 1930. Courtesy of Charlotte (Westwood) Lloyd Walkup.

Wounded Knee Battleground Store, which was burned during the 1973 occupation.

Extended Black Elk family. Front: Good Shell, Mrs. Black Elk (Anna Brings White), Ben's daughter Olivia, Black Elk. Rear: Ellen (Mrs. Ben) Black Elk, Ben, Nicholas Black Elk, Leo Looks Twice, Lucy Black Elk Looks Twice.

Ben and Ellen and children by their cabin home (Neihardt Papers).

Young men playing the hoop and spear game. The small building in the background had been newly installed for Black Elk's guests.

Hilda Neihardt, Black Elk, Chase-in-the-Morning, and John Neihardt, with hoops and spears for the hoop and spear game.

Raw liver is delicious fresh from the carcass! Iron Hawk, Fire Thunder, Standing Bear, and Red Elk. Neihardt is not shown, but he did eat a piece of the raw liver (Neihardt Papers).

Women begin work on the raw hide in front of our tepee.

Black Elk and Big Turnip at the traditional dance after the feast.

Standing Bear, Black Elk, and a friend.

Black Elk, Anna Brings White, and Holy Black Tail Deer.

Black Elk and Standing Bear as the holy man began telling his great vision.

Ben and Black Elk gesture to make a point during a typical interview scene. Enid, Black Elk, Ben, Standing Bear, and Neihardt.

John Neihardt and Standing Bear listen while Black Elk sings one of his many songs (Neihardt Papers).

seat their riders. Daddy promised we would go to a rodeo the first chance we had. That was something for very eager anticipation.

The next morning, May 9, we had a fine western breakfast in a local café, then started out for Pine Ridge Reservation and our journey's end—the home of Black Elk. We went through Gordon, Nebraska, where we saw *real* cowboys walking the streets—lean, weather-beaten men clad in worn jeans and tall boots, men who might easily have just stepped out of a movie at our little theater back home.

It is not easy to describe, though it is with me still, the feeling I had as we drove along gravel or dirt roads through the immense western country. For both Enid and me, it was a first. Although born in Nebraska, *eastern* Nebraska, I was so young when we moved to Missouri in 1920 that I did not recall anything about the plains country. Yet the plains of my birth were somehow part of me, and our dad's deep love for "the West" heightened the mysterious effect the "big country" had on me. The skies were so wide and so high and so blue. The very air seemed exciting and different, beyond its really being lighter and drier than our Missouri air.

I looked with intense emotion across wide patches of prairie to where an old windmill faithfully pumped water for animals and people. It was good to see deer grazing with cattle, or to be startled by a brightly colored pheasant in bulletlike flight before us. Truly we were in a new world that morning, and as I gazed at the barren landscape, I was enveloped in anticipation and a sense of promised adventure.

Because he was so imbued with the task he had embarked on, Daddy spoke much about the history of the country we passed through and, of course, the Indian people whose home it had been. He told us once more about Curly, Custer's Crow scout who had been Daddy's "brother friend." We recalled the small silver-colored metal box on the shelf by the clock at home, which held a large brass ring set with colored glass. This was the memento Curly had exchanged for a gold ring of my father's when the two pledged their brother-friendship.

Dad also told us about his friend Captain Grant Marsh, who commanded the steamboat *Far West,* which acted as the "navy" and supplied the needs of the army during the Indian wars. Many years later, Daddy had helped load that vessel. Perhaps most interesting of all was what Grant Marsh told him about how the news of the Custer massacre in the summer of 1876 was brought to him on the steamboat as it lay at anchor by the bank of the Missouri River in Montana.

Captain Marsh saw a husky Indian coming out of the bushes along the river, crying and tearing his hair. ("Crying and tearing his hair?" I asked. "Oh, yes," Daddy said, "Indian men did that!") While the battle was going on Custer had told Curly "save yourself," and Curly had lost no time in leaving, though he did hide for a time in a safe spot some distance away where he could watch the fighting. When he saw what happened, Curly rode swiftly toward the Missouri River, where Captain Marsh invited him aboard the *Far West*. The Crow scout told Marsh his story partly by drawing, for he did not speak much English.

Using his finger, Curly drew a large circle in the dust on the deck. In the middle he showed Custer's men, saying *"Absorika, Absorika* [our people, our people]." Then, all around the circle he jabbed with his fingers, saying over and over, "Sioux, Sioux, Sioux!" Then, clapping his hands together loudly, he breathed "Poof!" meaning it was all over. That, Captain Marsh told my father, was how the news of the death of General Custer and his men was brought to the white world.

We noticed a sign indicating the distance to Fort Robinson, and Daddy recalled his friend Major Lemly, who was stationed at the fort when Crazy Horse was killed there. The story of Crazy Horse's death as Lemly related it is told in *The Song of the Indian Wars*.

Telling about Crazy Horse reminded my father of the way the Indians fought on horseback. They rode in circles around the soldiers, each warrior hanging with one leg hooked over his pony's withers, leaning down and shooting with his short bow under his horse's neck. What a picture that created in my mind! And our dad, always ready with a poetic quotation, sharpened my mental picture with these lines from his *Song of the Indian Wars:*

There was no plain, just headgear bobbing in a toss of mane,
And horses, horses, horses plunging under.
Knee-deep in dust and thousand-footed thunder!

We passed through Rushville, Nebraska, and turned north toward Pine Ridge. The terrain was changing now, and eroded hills or ridges topped by dark pine trees appeared before us. To give expression to the compelling beauty of that broad panorama, Daddy chanted these lines newly written for his *Song of the Messiah:*

> There was a time when every gazing hill
> Was holy with the wonder that it saw,
> And every valley was a place of awe,
> And what the grass knew never could be told.

We listened, as always when Daddy recited, and for us too the lines intensified the beauty of the landscape.

When we reached Pine Ridge Reservation, we went first to the town of Pine Ridge and the agency office. My father had obtained permission from the secretary of the interior, Ray Lyman Wilbur, to spend time on the reservation and conduct interviews with Black Elk and the others. He had been told to report to the agent, Mr. Courtwright, who, Wilbur said, "would extend the usual courtesies." Whether the restriction was imposed by Agent Courtwright I do not know, but Enid's diary reveals that our stay on the reservation was to be limited to three weeks. Three weeks to conduct all that interviewing! It would put great pressure on the interviewer.

On the way from Pine Ridge to Manderson, we stopped at Wounded Knee, a small settlement near the site of the ill-famed Wounded Knee massacre. The old church was standing near the still unmarked mass grave, and our father told us something of what had occurred there in December 1890.

What a lonely, windswept place Wounded Knee was! Enid and I were duly impressed with its historical significance, but we were impatient to be on our way to Black Elk's home. So the three of us climbed back into the Gardner and drove the few remaining miles to Manderson.

Black Elk's Home
at Last

It was after noon on May 9 when we arrived at Manderson. It consisted mainly of an old log trading post and post office, a windmill with watering tank, hitching posts, and of course a collection of log cabins and houses. We parked at the trading post, and my dad went in to buy something for our lunch—by that time we were ravenous. I still remember what Daddy brought us: a sack of crackers and several small tins of little Vienna sausages. I thought this was a fabulous lunch, so different from the sit at the table variety. I had never seen little wienies in a can, and this memorable meal added to the feeling that we had embarked on a truly different experience. Since we ate in the car, it was a preview of today's drive-in restaurants.

Black Elk's two sons—Ben, who would be our interpreter, and Nicholas—were at the post, looking for some beds for us to sleep in. This surprised me, for we were planning to camp out.

Ben seemed like an older man to me, but he was about thirty. He was lean and muscular, of middle height, with aquiline features, a penetrating gaze, and protruding teeth. His shiny black hair, very straight, was cut short, in white man's style. He was not a handsome man but was very friendly and likeable, and he laughed often.

Nicholas I do not remember so well, because we did not see much of him that summer or in later years. He was about the same height as Ben, also slender, but he did not have the aquiline features so often considered typical of Indians. Nicholas had a roundish, more Oriental face. I think he must have looked more like his father while Ben, who looked quite different from the elder Black Elk, must have resembled his dead mother.

Except for the few we had passed on the roads and in the towns, I was seeing my first Indians. It is not surprising that I found their appearance strange and a bit frightening. I could not then have imagined how soon they would seem close to me, warm and friendly like part of the family.

Ben greeted us heartily and said that everybody was busy getting ready for us "out at the old man's place." Then he pointed out the road leading west from Manderson to Black Elk's home and told us to follow him. We did, Daddy driving behind Ben's old Ford along the dusty one-lane road.

And then—*then*—we were there!

Ben quickly drove up to the weathered, rectangular log house and began unloading the beds. We hesitated at the bottom of the low hill to take in the scene. Black Elk's cabin was partway up the rather barren hillside, and the grass surrounding it was still brown, though it was already May.

To the right of the cabin as we looked at it stood the pine shade Daddy had told us about, where he had first met with Black Elk the summer before. Because there were no trees to protect them from the hot sun, Black Elk's family had cut long poles and set them in the ground around the perimeter of what was to be the pine shade. Other poles were then placed over them to make the frame of a roof. Branches cut from pine trees and piled on top of these poles completed the bower, which did provide welcome coolness during the summer months.

Along the front and side of the cabin stood a number of small pine trees, and we later learned they had been cut and stuck in the ground to make the place look pretty for our arrival!

To the left and partway down the hill was a small building that seemed a bit surprised to be there. It was a privy, and judging by the fresh gash in the earth where it stood, we realized it had been placed there only recently, no doubt with our comfort and sensibilities in mind.

In front of Black Elk's cabin stood a well-worn wooden sledge drawn by a rough-coated horse. On it were a couple of wooden barrels, which two young Indian men were unloading and rolling into the house. They were bringing drinking water from White Horse Creek.

But something was missing from the scene. Where was the tepee that was to be our home while we were there? It was nowhere to be seen, and Enid and I asked, "But where will we *stay* while we're here? We didn't bring our tent."

"The tepee is probably just not ready yet," Daddy reassured us. "It will be all right. Don't worry."

The Gardner's engine roared, the gears clashed, and Daddy drove up to the cabin. As if in a dream, we stepped out and went in to meet our hosts.

Our Hosts,
the Black Elks

Members of the Black Elk family were bustling about the place, obviously getting things ready for their guests. They greeted us in a friendly way, but the two women, Ellen and Lucy, seemed as bashful as Enid and I felt. Daddy, after many years of association with Indians, and having met most of the family the year before, was quite at ease.

It was all completely new to me, and I can only remember standing in the background and looking—not rudely staring, but just taking in the rather stark interior of the cabin, with its woodstove, table and chairs, the big barrels of water that did not seem quite clean to me, and at one end of the room, some iron beds.

Ellen, Ben Black Elk's wife, was small, quiet and modest as an Indian woman should be, and very neat, with her long black hair worn in braids. She was of Mexican descent.

Black Elk's wife, Anna Brings White, was not at the cabin during our stay, except to help with preparations for the big feast. Perhaps she was staying at Ben's home with the children so Ellen would be free to help take care of Black Elk and us during the interviews.

Lucy, Black Elk's daughter and Ben's half-sister, was friendly, but for some reason I do not remember much about that first meeting except that I thought she was very pretty. Lucy was to become a very dear friend in later years.

One of the young men who had just rolled in a barrel of water caught my eye. He was of medium height, a bit stocky, and muscular. His black hair was intensely straight and cut short. His face was aquiline, and he seemed not to notice or care that on his right cheek there was a long smear of fresh blood. This was definitely *my* idea of what an Indian should look like! I remember being a little afraid of this young fellow who, except for his short hair, had to me all the bearing of a Sioux warrior. I was told that this was Leo Looks Twice, the new husband of Black Elk's daughter, Lucy, and somehow I got the impression that Black Elk did not entirely approve of his son-in-law. Leo had a dashing manner and was very friendly. He appealed to me, but in a scary way.

We didn't need to be told that the older man who greeted us kindly in Lakota was Black Elk. His was not an aquiline face; its shape reminded me of pictures I had seen of Orientals. His skin was almost black, and I later learned he was so dark because he worked outdoors much of the time.

Black Elk was of medium height (I have since been told by a great-grandson that he was five feet, eight inches tall). He had the somewhat gaunt but strong frame of one who has lived a hard life and done many things. His graying hair was cut short, and he wore a rumpled white man's suit, complete with tie. His eyes had a strange appearance, and my father told us later that he suffered from glaucoma, which had left him nearly blind.

Black Elk was just sixty-eight years old at the time, but to us teenagers he seemed ancient. Although he did not then, or at any time while we were with him, speak directly to me, I did not feel uncomfortable in his presence, nor did I feel ignored. This was the mysterious holy man of the Oglalas who had been central in our thoughts for the past months, and we regarded him, fittingly, with more than a touch of awe.

But beyond that, Black Elk seemed to Enid and me much like someone's grandfather. When I think myself back to 1931 and try to recall our feelings in his presence, I can best express them by saying we thought he was very kind and "sweet." Yes, that's about it: Black Elk carried an aura of kindness, sweetness, mixed with more than a touch of sadness.

Ben and Nicholas had brought in the beds they had obtained in Manderson, and we learned from Ben why they were needed. "It's too cold for you to camp out, John," he said, "and the wimmens say you and the girls have to sleep in the house. We will sleep outside." "No, Ben, you will not sleep outside. We will *all* sleep in the cabin." And so it was. A blanket was hung from the low ceiling to make two rooms— one for the Neihardts and one for the Black Elks.

Enid reports that first evening in her diary: "We had a fine supper at Black Elk's and then hurried to bed. We lay down with our Indian blankets covering us, and we were going to sleep in an oblong house, not in a tepee which is round! We kept our clothes on every night—we had heard that Braves always slept with their clothes on."

We could scarcely have expected to feel at home in the cabin, but we did feel that we were with good people who would be our friends. We slept well that first night.

The Interviews Begin

"Come and get it or we'll throw it out!" Ben grinned as he announced breakfast the next morning, and many times thereafter we would hear this hearty invitation to a meal. I doubt Ben ever had to call a second time. We were always hungry, and Ellen and Lucy cooked the good, plain food we liked as well as a few Indian specialties, which for the most part we also enjoyed.

After a good breakfast, Daddy discussed food arrangements with Ellen. While we were with the Black Elks, my father would provide money for provisions for all, and so on this first morning he gave Ellen what she said she would need for the next day or so.

Black Elk had invited some of his best friends to join in the talks, as he and my father had planned, and the fine old men arrived promptly —Iron Hawk, Fire Thunder, Standing Bear, Chase-in-the-Morning, and Holy Black Tail Deer. There was an air of high expectancy as Black Elk, these five old warriors, Ben, my sister Enid, and my father went into the pine shade to begin the interviews. Blankets were spread on the bare ground where the participants sat, arranging themselves in a circle with Ben, the interpreter, between Black Elk and my father. As designated "official observer," I quietly took a place nearby.

Black Elk had previously requested that his son Ben act as interpreter, because he felt confident Ben would translate honestly—would repeat in English (of which Black Elk understood very little) just what Black Elk said. He also asked that Standing Bear be present during all the interviews, because the presence of his longtime friend would make it clear to Neihardt that he was telling the truth. Communicating "the truth" was important to Black Elk, and this arrangement was calculated to achieve that result.

It was May 10, 1931, and I wonder now if anyone in our group fully realized the historic importance of the interviews that would take place during the succeeding days. The book that would come out of those talks was destined to go around the world and be an inspiration to many, as well as a storehouse of Native American culture used by Indians and whites alike. But let us not waste time wondering: the important thing now is telling what happened.

My father began by passing around cigarettes. While the old men smoked, my father opened the discussions with brief remarks intended to give a background for what he hoped the interviews would reveal. He also assured the men that they would be paid for their time at a rate Black Elk and Ben had suggested. Just what the daily stipend was I probably never knew. By today's standards I am sure it would seem small, but to those good men it was welcome and well received.

As my father spoke, waited for Ben to interpret in Lakota, then continued speaking, I looked around the circle, and in the intensity of the moment what I saw was stamped on my memory. All the men were dressed in white men's clothing on that day, and several wore cowboy hats. Fire Thunder was the oldest, but he was still slim and strongly built, as was deep-chested Iron Hawk, and I thought how powerful they must have been as young warriors. Standing Bear was one of the most memorable for me. In him the stereotype of the dignified Indian became real. Tall and straight in spite of his seventy-two years and the hard work he had done, Standing Bear was kingly. When he walked into a group—even when we sat out on the prairie—Standing Bear had the imposing bearing of a monarch. A member of the Minneconjoux tribe, he was Black Elk's most trusted friend. They had been friends since boyhood.

Holy Black Tail Deer was also a good-looking man, with long braids, but I do not remember much more about him. I believe he was a relative, for he appears in family pictures.

But Chase-in-the-Morning! He had to be one of the handsomest men Enid and I had ever seen, though he was certainly not young. Not as tall as Standing Bear, Chase-in-the-Morning was slim, hardened, and strongly built; his bowed legs attested to many years on horseback. His aquiline face, twinkling eyes, and long hair completed for us the picture of the perfect Indian. He was friendly and fun-loving, and we communicated well with him in spite of our language differences.

Ben and the "old man," Black Elk, I have already described. As for my father, I have mentioned that he was not a large man, but he was very strong, very intense, with wavy blond hair that had darkened to a sandy brown and bright blue eyes that revealed his enthusiasm for the job he had undertaken. With a background of some thirty years of friendship with the Omaha and Sioux peoples, during which he had gained an appreciation for them and for their cultures that was rare indeed in those times, he was ideally suited for the task at hand. That Black Elk had intuitively known this about Neihardt on their first meeting proved to be the remarkable beginning of this whole story.

Enid was nineteen, taller than I and pretty, with blue eyes and wavy blond hair. Trained as a stenographer, she was well prepared to act as reporter for the interviews. Enid had a friendly, easy way that must have endeared her to our hosts. My, she did like those handsome Indians! But we all did, for they were easy to like.

The raconteurs present introduced themselves and told something about their lives. I shall not repeat those introductions here, for I do not remember them, but they are all in Enid's transcribed notes or in *Black Elk Speaks*.

In the original telling their stories were disconnected, and Ben's interpreting had to be interrupted often as my father made certain that what the old men said was coming through correctly. When they spoke of historical matters, my father was greatly assisted because, after many years of research, he was familiar with most of the history. It was not easy for Ben—this was his first effort as an interpreter—but it would become still more difficult when Black Elk told about matters of which his son, and my father as well, had heard little or nothing before.

The Indians, my dad, and Enid soon got into the swing of things, and this is how I remember they handled the interviews. It was similar to the way things proceeded when I acted as reporter for my father in 1944 when he again talked with Black Elk and another old Sioux named Eagle Elk. One of the old men spoke in Lakota for a few minutes, then Ben translated, into English, haltingly at first. If the meaning was unclear, Neihardt questioned, then Ben repeated the question to the storyteller and waited for his response. When that particular portion of the story was understandable my father repeated it, Ben said "that's it," and Enid recorded it in her shorthand book. If there was no problem with understanding what the teller was saying, Enid recorded it immediately. To one not directly involved, however, the stories did seem slow in coming; at times the interviewing process seemed tedious.

Interlude at Chadron:
"These Many Grasses . . ."

We had to interrupt our interviews on May 11, for another lecture had been scheduled, this time at Nebraska State College in Chadron. The road to Chadron was beautiful, and on the way we saw something new to Enid and me—prairie-dog towns. Hundreds of the funny little animals were sitting up very straight in front of their homes or scurrying about, just being prairie dogs. On the way to Chadron, Daddy killed two prairie chickens with his nine-shot Smith and Wesson revolver.

Quite a marksman and hunter, he had decided years before that hunting with a shotgun was too easy. Recently he had switched to a pistol for the same reason: a rifle was too easy to be sportsmanlike. During our stay with the Black Elk family, he greatly impressed Ben with his ability to hit a chicken or pheasant at ninety yards. He was shooting right up to the capability of the K-9 revolver, that's for sure.

When we reached Chadron, we stopped at a cabin camp and decided to have the prairie chickens for dinner, "stew fried" as Daddy liked them. Well the birds were old and tough, and it was apparent they would be a long time cooking, so we went to a movie in town while they simmered slowly. When we returned we ate hurriedly, for we did not like the cabin: it was not at all clean. For this reason, and because it would be easier to make ourselves presentable for the lecture in better quarters, we went into Chadron and took two rooms at a hotel.

Daddy's lecture at the college was another success. After reading several of his lyrics in his powerful style (he could project his voice so that it easily filled an auditorium without a loudspeaker), Daddy announced that he would read "The Death of Crazy Horse" from his *Song of the Indian Wars*. He recited the story of that great man's death, and there were few dry eyes in the house as he intoned the last lines:

Who knows the crumbling summit where he lies,
Alone among the badlands? Kiotes prowl
About it, and the voices of the owl
Assume the day-long sorrow of the crows,
These many grasses and these many snows.

Though Enid and I did not much like it, we were asked to sit on the stage during the program. I recall having considerable difficulty keeping my dress down over my knees while sitting on a straight chair before all those people. After the performance came the usual handshaking, but by this time we were used to it and didn't mind. A sorority picnic, a tour of a Nebraska state park, and a pleasant overnight stay at the home of one of the professors topped off our visit to Chadron. On May 13 we left for Manderson, on our way seeing more of the country we thought so beautiful.

A Home of Our
Own at Last

When we reached Black Elk's cabin, the first thing we saw was our tepee, and we were told Iron Hawk had put it up for us. It was a wonderful sight: made of heavy white cloth something like canvas, it was painted in the traditional "sacred" way with Indian symbols, among them a beautiful high-headed horse that stood proudly on the front. Over the entrance to the tepee was a rainbow, which would have special meaning to us as we learned about Black Elk's vision. No doubt Black Elk had directed what should be depicted.

We were very happy, for now we had a home of our own. We moved our blankets and other belongings out of the cabin, and that night we slept for the first time in a real tepee. It was truly a momentous event for the three of us, and we did sleep especially well. There is something about sleeping right on Mother Earth that is rejuvenating. I believe that somehow our bodies receive strength or power from the ground. I do feel, when I am lying on the earth, that my vitality is being restored—that my batteries are being charged.

The next day, May 14, interviews began again, this time in the tepee. The "cast" sat cross-legged in a circle, on blankets laid on the dirt floor. Unfortunately on this day the interviews were interrupted again, this time by a new excitement.

A few days before, Daddy had told Ben and the others that he would like to host with them a real old-time Indian feast. The Black Elk family had been making preparations ever since, and getting the word out that everyone in the area was invited. I do not know how the invitations were extended, but it proved effective.

From their herd of cattle Lucy and Leo chose a fine young beef animal, which they sold to Daddy for the occasion. Black Elk, Standing Bear, Red Elk, Fire Thunder, and Iron Hawk butchered the Holstein bull in the approved way. After removing the skin and opening up the animal, they cut the still-warm liver in small pieces and passed it around. I can see those old men yet, each with a knife in his hand, cutting off small pieces of liver, still dripping blood, and eating them with evident relish. Daddy ate one piece, declared it was *ever* so good, but declined more. Enid and I did not eat any.

In the meantime several old women had come, among them Mrs. Black Elk, and they set about scraping the hide, which they had staked out on the ground near our tepee. I remember being rather afraid of those old ladies. Their hair was in long braids; they wore long, dark, shapeless dresses that came to the ground, and each had a belt from which hung a sheath for a large butcher knife. They seemed always to have those big knives with them, and that, together with their serious, rather severe demeanor, caused me to take the long route around them whenever I came near where they were working.

I thought the women did not like me, and now I realize they may well have disapproved of *my* demeanor, wearing breeches as I did and being free to ride with Leo and others and generally go about as I pleased. I don't think I was loud or boisterous, and I certainly felt very respectful, but they may well have thought the freedom I enjoyed was not appropriate for a young girl. Now that I think of it, some of the neighbor ladies back home in Branson thought the same thing! Young girls there were also not generally permitted the wholesome outdoor freedom our parents encouraged.

That afternoon we played with hoops and spears that Iron Hawk had made while we were away. The hoops were formed from small limbs or young tree shoots bent into a circle, then secured with leather thongs. Across the hoops, additional thongs were loosely woven so as to leave openings for the long straight sticks thrown by the players. Two teams were chosen. A player on one side threw the hoop sharply downward in front of him so that it rolled swiftly toward the other team, who ran alongside it and threw their spears, trying to get one through the hoop. It was a surprisingly fast game, for those young men could really run, even wearing cowboy boots and—yes!—the omnipresent cowboy hats. We really liked the game, and all of us took part, even Black Elk and Chase-in-the-Morning.

We learned that in the old days this game provided another kind of entertainment—a sort of gambling. For example, a mark would be put beside one of the open spaces in the interwoven rawhide strips that would indicate a prize—perhaps a horse. If one of the players should happen to drive his spear into this particular opening, he would win the horse!

Meanwhile the women were preparing food for the great feast, and Enid and I drove to Manderson more than once to get supplies, particularly all the dried peaches, raisins, and prunes we could find, which were stewed into a kind of thick sauce. The meat was cut up, and all was ready for the big day.

An Old-Time Feast

Right after breakfast the next morning, we all offered to help get ready for the feast. Red Elk had made a tripod of small saplings, over which he hung the paunch of the beef animal filled with water. On a nearby fire he heated rocks, then dropped them into the water, making it boil. The beef, cut into small chunks, followed. Red Elk was making that Sioux favorite, soup. Ellen and Lucy were busily stirring up the thick sauce they had made from the dried peaches, raisins, and prunes. There were many loaves of bread, but I do not remember seeing the fry bread that is so popular today. It may be a recent introduction into Sioux life. Tables were set up for preparing and displaying the food, and soon all was ready for the big celebration.

Guests began to arrive, on horseback or in wagons, and they politely waited for a while in the little valley below the house. One couple who came to the feast stands out in my memory, for the man was the largest person I had ever seen. So large he was—so wide—that he had to sit on the wagon seat alone while his wife sat on a straight chair in the wagon box. He was not particularly fat—just *big*. Ben told me his name, but it is long forgotten.

Except for a reporter from the Lincoln *Journal,* the guests were all Sioux who lived on the reservation. There was one other uninvited white person—a rather obsequious man who came up to my father and, in a confidential tone, told him that he could supply plenty of liquor and would share the profits with him. I had not often seen my father so angry—he told that man, in strong language the poor fellow could understand only too well, that he had better get out of there right away! Obviously surprised and taken quite off guard, the man hastened to his car, parked at the bottom of the hill. "If you come back," Daddy called after him, "I'll have you arrested!" The liquor merchant did not return, and the feast was undisturbed by any such unsympathetic white influence.

It was a tremendous job for Ellen and Lucy, helped by several other women and men, to get the food ready for the two or three hundred people who were expected for the feast. We were happily surprised at how many did come. I do not recall that any except the reporter and the liquor promoter came in automobiles. Horses and wagons were left at the bottom of the hill, where a number of small trees provided shade and hitching posts. Then the guests came up to the cabin, standing or sitting wherever they wished, for there was space aplenty on that barren hill.

The older, traditional Indians, including the men who were taking part in the interviews, were dressed in their best ceremonial clothing. Black Elk's attire was simple, as befitted a holy man: he wore a tight-fitting fur headpiece from which hung a single eagle feather, a simple tunic decorated with a porcupine-quill breastplate, trousers, and beaded moccasins. He carried a coup stick bound with leather and fur. Standing Bear and Chase-in-the-Morning wore brightly colored feather headdresses, and their clothing was of deerskin. Other older men were similarly dressed, and they made a most striking appearance. Younger men wore trousers or jeans, shirts, and cowboy hats and boots. The older women too were dressed in ceremonial garb— long deerskin or cowhide dresses and much fancy beadwork. And, of course, belts around their waists, from which hung that most important accessory, a *knife*.

When preparations were complete the people were told, and the feast began. Guests—upward of three hundred—sat on the ground in a large circle that began at the cabin and then went down the hill, along its base, and up the hill again. Each person had brought a bowl or plate, some utensils, and a cup. All waited politely until served by a number of young men, perhaps twelve to fifteen years old, who carried the food around the large circle, giving each person soup, meat, fruit pudding, bread, and hot coffee. The coffee was prepared in big kettles on an open fire, and plenty of sugar was added during the brewing. I did not drink coffee yet, but my father did, and though he didn't care for sugar, he made no complaints.

I had not attended any kind of feast before that day, let alone one for so many people, but it was not the size of the event that impressed me most, it was the courtesy of all involved. *Such polite people,* I thought. Everything proceeded in proper order, with real dignity. Although I don't remember eating anything myself, I'm sure I did. However, I never could forget the respect I had for those Sioux or the affection I felt for them. Never.

The feast was over, but there was more to come. The guests were told that there would be an adoption and naming ceremony, and they gathered around Standing Bear and Black Elk, who conducted the ceremony in the traditional way. I do not remember the details, but my father, in a letter written a few days later to his biographer, Julius T. House, called it a "rather impressive ceremony." We three Neihardts were officially taken into the Oglala tribe and given names that my father referred to in his letter as "holy names, taken from Black Elk's vision."

We were called up in order for the ceremony. First they named Enid, and she was very happy with her name: Ta-Sa-Ge-a-Luta-Win, which Ben translated as She Who Walks with Her Holy Red Staff. The name meant that she would be happily married and have plenty.

The name I was given has had deep significance for me all my life: Unpo Wichachpi Win, or Daybreak Star Woman. Black Elk explained that name by saying I had a great desire to learn and that wisdom comes to one who rises early and sees the daybreak star. My father later said he wondered how the holy man could recognize the different natures of my sister and me, or know I had a studious bent. Certainly I had no books with me.

The name Black Elk had chosen for my father was Peta-Wigamou-Gke, which Ben translated as Flaming Rainbow. Black Elk explained the reason for that name: "This world is like a garden," he said, "and over this garden his words go like rain. Where they fall, they leave everything a little greener. And after his words have passed, the memory of them shall stand long in the west like a flaming rainbow." Black Elk was quiet for a moment, then he added, "Whenever in the future I see a rainbow, I will think of my friend Mr. Neihardt."

Then all three of us were advised that perhaps sometime we might need something, or the tribe might. Then either would help the other. Deeply impressed, we agreed.

After some cleanup chores, when it was nearly dark (Enid's diary said "about nine o'clock"), everyone gathered at a place that had been prepared for dancing. In the middle of the circular dance area, a pole was set up with an American flag flying. Four young men, dressed in ordinary white men's shirts and trousers, each wearing a big hat, stood around a bass drum that they held up off the ground. The men had padded drumsticks, and as they sang for the dance, all four beat the drum in the rhythm required for the particular song or dance. This is how it is done today at powwows, except that the singers and drummers are often seated.

Then a young man wearing a headdress and with bells on his ankles—"the starter"—did just that: he initiated the dance, going around the circle clockwise a time or two by himself, the bells on his ankles jingling as he placed his feet on the ground—toe, heel, toe, heel.

Then the old "longhairs" dressed in full regalia danced their traditional ceremonial and war dances, and the women stood around the edge of the circle, rising on their toes and sinking down again to the beat of the drum. Children gathered nearby, including Olivia, Ben's little four-year-old with the big dark eyes. (I thought the Indian children were so beautiful!) We were caught up in the beauty and the excitement of the singing and the beating of the drum. I still cannot hear Indian singing and drumming without wanting to join in the dance, and when it is appropriate I do!

As the dancing was about to begin, we noted that two horsebacks were just coming over the horizon to the east. They were Enid and a young Sioux who had asked her to ride with him. They arrived, dismounted, and joined the crowd around the dance area.

After the old-timers' ceremonial dancing, it was announced that next there would be a rabbit dance, a social dance for both men and women. Many of the songs sung for the rabbit dance had pretty melodies, and I remember one or two today. In the rabbit dance a man and a woman dance side by side, holding hands much as we do in social dancing, except that they do not face each other. The rhythm of the drums was one-*two*, one-*two*, and the dancers moved two steps forward and one step back, around and around in a circle, until the song ended and the drumming stopped. Enid danced with a couple of the young men, and I was asked to dance by none other than Chase-in-the-Morning. Imagine that if you can!

My father had protested that he never danced, but two substantial Indian women decided this would not do. Each took one of his hands, and together they pulled him over to the dance area. It was a hilarious sight, seeing my father dancing with those women, his arms barely reaching across their broad backs. It was all in fun, and everyone laughed heartily, even Daddy.

During the dance, the young men who did the drumming sang this song in English:

Oh yes, I love ya honey, bunny, boy;
I don't care if you're married, I still love ya.
I'll get you yet, Hey-o-ha! Hey-o-ha!

Since they laughed, as we all did, when they sang it, I have always considered it a take-off on white people's songs, as it might well be.

Although I understand that in the old days Indians often feasted and danced all night long, about midnight or shortly after everyone went home, and we started for our tepee. As we neared the tepee Leo came up and asked, "Hilda, do you want to ride-out in the morning? I saw some wild horses over there." He motioned with his shoulder to show that the horses were west of the cabin. "The old folks will be tired and won't get up very early in the morning anyway. We can leave at daybreak."

It had been a wonderful, memorable day, and now the next day promised a new kind of excitement. Did I want to go chasing wild horses with Leo? What a question!

Black Elk Begins the Great Vision

When Leo and I returned from our ride, breakfast was in progress. Our early morning adventure had made us ravenous, and we gladly accepted Ellen's invitation to eat. Sitting together at table in the cabin, we told about seeing the herd of wild horses and how we could not get close enough even to *think* of catching one. Ben advised, "You can't catch the wild ones that way. I've always known that you have to plan so they don't see you first. Those ponies are smart and never miss much. Leo, you're just going to have to try another way!" "Perhaps another time," Leo responded. I'm sure, however, that everyone knew Leo wasn't really trying to catch any horses; he was just showing me an exciting time.

The talks resumed in our tepee after the late breakfast. On this day, May 16, the day after the big feast, everyone was tired, but the important business of interviewing went on in spite of the weariness.

Black Elk said he would continue the telling of his great vision, which he had begun after our return from Chadron and which had been interrupted by the old-time feast and the extensive preparations for that great event. But a change would have to be made; the talks must be moved, he said, to Standing Bear's land, because his telling of the vision must not be heard by anyone except his son Ben, his lifelong friend Standing Bear, and the three of us. Black Elk explained that it was a sacred thing he would be relating, and he added that he had previously told the whole of the vision to no one, not even his son or Standing Bear.

Mrs. Standing Bear, born Louisa Renick, was a well-educated

Viennese woman from a well-to-do family. Standing Bear had met her when he was hospitalized in Vienna during his tour with the Buffalo Bill Wild West Show. Like many young ladies of her station in life, Louisa was a volunteer at the hospital. She and the tall, handsome young Minneconjoux became acquainted and fell in love. After Standing Bear returned to America, she followed him. They married, and she lived the hard reservation life with him until his death in 1934.

The Standing Bears lived in a large log house that had been painted white. "A *real* house," Enid described it in her diary. Their house had ceilings inside and a shingle roof—the only house on the reservation with a shingle roof at that time, I was told. Black Elk's cabin was of unpainted logs and had a sod roof from which weeds and grass grew. The Standing Bears had a large garden, chickens, and a milk cow as well as horses and a herd of beef cattle. A time or two Standing Bear came to our tepee in the early morning and, in his grand manner, presented Enid with a pint of fresh milk. This was a great treat for Enid and me, because milk was scarce. We did occasionally have butter.

I remember feeling considerable sympathy for Mrs. Standing Bear, because she looked work-worn. Years later I met the great-grandson of Standing Bear, the artist Arthur Amiotte, and he told me that his great-grandfather was a subchief and that he and his wife did work very hard because they felt responsible to provide some of the food tribal members needed. Mrs. Standing Bear corresponded for a time in German with my mother, who said that her letters showed she was very well educated.

As Black Elk wished, the interviews resumed in a grassy spot near some small trees on the Standing Bear land. We placed cotton "Indian" blankets on the ground and built a small fire nearby to provide for ceremonies such as the burning of sage and sweet grass and the lighting of the pipe.

I also used the fire to prepare our noon meal. Over that tiny fire I cooked potatoes, vegetables, meat if any was available, and my specialty—golden cornbread. I knew well that nothing should be burned, everything must be clean, and especially, there should be no ashes in the food! Daddy was a meticulous camper, and I had learned from him.

Black Elk's story continued, and we learned that when he was very young, strange things began happening to him: he could understand the birds when they talked together, he received messages from them, and he often had a strange feeling that he was being called by someone. Then, when he was nine years old, his great vision happened. I remember how intently I listened to his telling of it, for I had also experienced vivid dreams. They were not like Black Elk's vision, of course, but they did prepare me for what I would hear. I was already a believer.

Black Elk and Standing Bear were good friends at the time of his vision, and Standing Bear contributed his memories of the illness that came upon the young Black Elk, telling how the small boy was carried on a travois after his legs crumpled under him and he could not ride. He remembered the days when Black Elk lay in his parents' tepee and was thought dead, and he recalled the "cure" that occurred when he awoke from the vision. That cure was attributed to Whirlwind Chaser, whom Black Elk's parents had hired to treat their sick boy, and he was given a horse as payment.

During the telling of the vision, there were many songs. It seemed to me that Indians must have a song for everything, and I guess they did. Black Elk would often interrupt his story, say "there was a song for that," and then take up his drum. To a very fast, even beat, he would sing in his none-too-melodious voice. Sometimes there was a recognizable tune, at other times the words were carried in a chant. But the words were often poetic, and we used some of them in a song. One in particular has been meaningful to us, and I quote it in a later chapter.

Often during the telling the old man would tire and, without explanation, simply put his head down on the blanket and go to sleep. While he slept, the rest of us might nap also, or perhaps walk around and visit.

I recall that when we were passing the time during one such interlude my father—all the while pacing up and down in his characteristic vigorous manner—declared to us: "I just *cannot believe* the beauty and the meaning of what is coming out of that old man's head. I know of no other vision in religious literature that is the equal of this!" Later, in a letter to a friend, he described the vision as "a marvelous thing, vast in extent, full of profound significance and perfectly formed. If it were literature instead of a dance ritual, it would be a literary masterpiece!"

Once while out riding with my father, Ben—overcome by the powerful newness and beauty of what his father was recounting—exclaimed to my father, "Isn't it great? Isn't it *wonderful?*"

"What is wonderful, Ben?"

"What the old man is a-sayin'. I always knew he had *something,* but I didn't know what in hell it was!"

Although the overall tone during the telling of the great vision was serious, there were humorous times as well. On one occasion Black Elk was telling about the power of the west and the spirits who live in that quarter. Referring to those spirits, Ben interpreted, "thunder beans." My father, not immediately understanding, asked, "thunder beans?" To which query Ben, with that familiar piercing look on his sharp face that so often reflected his eagerness to get his father's meaning across, replied, "Yes, you know; you're a *bean,* and *I'm* a bean." My dad understood and clarified for Enid: "Oh, I see—thunder *beings.*" "Yes," Ben replied, "thunder beans." Now we understood each other!

On this day everyone, including Black Elk, was tired after the feast and the dancing of the day before, so the interviewing was stopped in late afternoon. This let Enid accept an invitation to go horseback riding, which she dearly loved, and I was asked to go along. I was ready to ride out again even after my morning's jaunt with Leo. On this day we rode in daylight, but sometimes because of the long working sessions we rode at night, accompanied by Leo and other young Lakotas.

After we returned, we had another good supper with the family. It was late, and all of us were quite ready to go to bed. After a good drink of water from the dipper that hung near the barrel in the cabin, we did just that.

Another sound sleep on Mother Earth in our round tepee made the three of us ready for another day. We eagerly anticipated learning more about Black Elk's great vision. As Enid confided to her diary, "Black Elk is not very good at telling history, but he is very good at telling his vision."

How It Was

Since my father had been allowed only three weeks to get his story, it was necessary to work long hours on the interviews. Although he did like to have some free time for fun such as hunting or riding, for the most part the talks continued from early morning until late into the evening—often ten or eleven o'clock. At night a kerosene lantern provided light, and Enid sat near it to see what she was writing.

Both Enid and I loved to ride horseback, and when we were free Leo and other young men invited us to go with them. Sometimes we rode at night, because the days were so crowded with work. Daddy remarked in a letter to a friend that he would have been "reluctant to let us go out like that with the white boys at home," but the young Indian men were polite and respectful, and he felt we were safe with them. Well, he was right; we *were*. Of course, I was just a tomboyish kid, and one might have expected them to treat me in big-brotherly fashion. But Enid was nineteen, a very pretty young woman, and she was never made uncomfortable when she rode with one of those young fellows. The Sioux are truly handsome people, and I am sure my older sister was more than a little infatuated with those fine young men.

Once Leo, Enid, some others, and I rode past White Horse Creek at night. The horses were thirsty, so we let them drink from the dark water of the stream. Leo asked, "Want a drink?" Then he dismounted, threw himself down by the edge of the stream, put his face to the water, and drank. To Enid and me drinking at night from an unfamiliar stream without being able to see the water seemed a bit adventuresome, but trusting Leo we also drank, and the water tasted good. After all, I reminded myself, it was the same water we were using at the cabin.

When we had remounted Leo told us, "You know, Crazy Horse is supposed to be buried someplace near here. The old man said so, but I don't think he knows just where the grave is." Learning that we might be near the grave of that great Sioux hero, of whom Enid and I had heard so much from Daddy, added greatly to the mystical feeling that already permeated our night ride.

I remember coming back from that ride and from a distance seeing our tepee glowing in the darkness, a golden triangle against the night sky, out in that vast loneliness. We stopped our horses and just stood looking for a few minutes. For Enid and me, of course, the lighted tepee was a strangely beautiful sight, but I wonder if it was not even more so for those young Indian men. What thoughts might they have had of a life that was gone forever?

Back at the cabin, Enid and I unsaddled our horses, then turned them loose on the range. When we reached our tepee, we found Daddy and Ben inside, making plans.

The next day, after a hearty breakfast, the interviews resumed. The work proceeded regularly, and it *was* work. I recall how slow it all seemed at times, but there were also exciting or amusing episodes. Since I went riding out with Leo Looks Twice several times, I did miss part of the interviews on those days, but I was there most of the time, performing my duties as official observer and, when we were away from Black Elk's cabin, as camp cook.

While interviews were conducted at Black Elk's place, we ate the noon meal with his family, and Ellen or Lucy would let us know when it was ready. More than once Ellen bashfully, respectfully, asked my father, "Is it all right if I invite them to eat with us?" She would indicate some Indians who had arrived by wagon or on horseback, who sat politely halfway down the hill, their backs to the cabin. (Oh, no! they weren't thinking it was mealtime!) Of course my father agreed, so we often had a large group of people at a meal. Much as we enjoyed their company, and much as he wanted to behave in accordance with Sioux custom, it did become expensive for him to feed so many, even welcome guests! The small advance he had received from Morrow was melting like ice in summertime, and he feared his funds would not last through the interviews.

There was more privacy and less feasting after the move to Standing Bear's land. Enid understood the problem and exaggerated to her diary, "Daddy has to feed the whole Sioux Nation!"

Having so many guests meant we needed extra food from the Manderson trading post, and since I was only the official observer, I was often sent to fetch something Ellen or Lucy needed. I saddled a faithful little spotted mare called Daisy and trotted off down the dusty road. It was empty country, and I rarely met anyone on the way. At Manderson I tied my horse at the hitching rack outside the store, bought the groceries, tied the cloth sack Ellen provided for them to the saddle, and galloped home. Everything was as romantic as the western stories I loved to read —hitching rack, log store, dust, and all.

It is so brightly stored in my memory: Can it be that all this happened sixty years ago?

The Sacred Hoop

Because his power as a holy man had come from the west and from the thunder beings who live there, it was apparent that Black Elk always felt a special involvement with those beings. In our family too we feel a kinship with the thunder beings, and when a big storm is approaching we often call out, as we learned to do from Black Elk: "Hey-a-hey! Hey-a-hey!" There is a deep joy that comes from feeling oneness with our surroundings, from the sense of belonging to the powers that envelop us. That joy makes any fear seem needless.

Although the recorded reminiscences of Black Elk and his friends are poignantly interesting and historically valuable, undoubtedly the most remarkable telling and the most meaningful revelations in all the interviews are found in the great vision that was given to Black Elk as a boy. Neihardt expressed this opinion shortly after he met with Black Elk, saying in a letter, "The principal part of his story is the vision which he had at the age of nine and which seems to have lasted during twelve days of unconsciousness. This vision is a marvelous thing."

More than once Black Elk told us something about the sacred hoop, a symbol that is of particular importance for understanding his vision. The deceptively simple concept of the hoop of the people, the sacred hoop, impressed me so deeply as the holy man told it that it has been a guiding influence throughout my life.

The sacred hoop, we learned during those days in 1931, is a religious concept that grew out of the thoughts of people who lived close to the earth, who could and did look about themselves and see that they, all living things, and the earth they called Mother were part of a vast system that included in its mystery the winds, the sun, the moon, and the stars. I listened—we all did—with rapt attention and felt the power in his words as Black Elk told about this great hoop. Now after many years I am able to realize at least partially how filled with beauty and practical meaning is this simple concept.

Today, in a culture that typically thinks of learning and spiritual values mainly as they may be developed or found in technological institutions, one might well feel awestruck that this enlightening idea of the sacred hoop, which could be a spiritual model for a better life on this earth, was developed by people who sat cross-legged on buffalo robes or blankets in simple tepees on the prairie. To understand this, one must keep in mind that as Black Elk spoke we were learning about things of the spirit out of a culture that, though undeveloped technologically, was advanced in other important ways.

We—Black Elk, Ben, Standing Bear, my father, Enid, and I—were seated on blankets spread on the grass of Standing Bear's land on the Pine Ridge Reservation in South Dakota. A few straggling clumps of chokecherry or plum brush behind us gave some shade from the midday sun. A small fire, from which the sacred pipe would be lit, smoldered nearby. The old holy man was getting ready to tell about his great vision, and the hoop of the universe would be important background for that telling.

As he spoke, Black Elk raised his arms and held them before him to represent a great circle, and Ben earnestly and at times haltingly explained in English what the old man said. It all came together something like this.

"Imagine a hoop so large that everything is in it—all two-leggeds like us, the four-leggeds, the fish of the streams, the wings of the air, and all green things that grow. Everything is together in this great hoop.

"Across this hoop, running from the east where the days of men begin to the west where the days of men end, is the hard black road of worldly difficulties. We all must pass along this road, for it represents the world of everyday life."

Black Elk thought a bit, then commented, "It is not easy to live in this world."

We had accepted that simple truth when he continued: "If that black road were the only one along which we might pass, then this life would not mean much; but there is another road. It is the good red road of spiritual understanding, and it begins in the south where lives the power to grow and proceeds to the north, the region of white hairs and death.

"Where this good red road crosses the hard black road, *that place is holy,* and there springs the sacred tree that shall fill with leaves and blooms and singing birds."

Throughout his description, Black Elk had gestured to indicate the directions the two roads run, and when he spoke of the tree, he raised both arms to show how high that great tree rose into the air.

Once more the holy man grew quiet and thoughtful, then he said simply: "And that is the sacred hoop. The power for everything an Indian does comes from the sacred hoop, and the power will not work in anything but a circle. Everything is now too square. The sacred hoop is vanishing among the people."

We were quiet, for we sensed that Black Elk was not finished. He continued: "To understand the hoop, we must speak of the four quarters of the universe and the six directions. You will remember I told you how the sacred pipe is offered in prayer. This is how it should be done."

Leaning down to the small fire that smoldered in front of us, Standing Bear lit the pipe and passed it to Black Elk, who took it and continued:

"Holding the pipe in the right hand—so—we begin by offering the mouthpiece to the west, where the thunder beings live. The color for the west is blue or black, and because the thunder beings have the power to make live or to destroy, the symbols that represent the west are a cup of water and a bow and arrows.

"We then proceed around the hoop to the north, where the great white giant lives in power and whence come the great white cleansing winds. The symbols for the north are the sacred white wind, the white goose's wing, and a sacred herb, and the color for this quarter is white.

"Next we offer the pipe to the power of the east, whence comes the light of day and where the daybreak star lives. From the light of the east come wisdom and understanding, and from understanding, peace. The symbols of the east are the daybreak star and the pipe, and the color for this quarter is red.

"From the east, we go again to the right and offer the pipe to the south, whence come the summer and the power to grow. The color for this quarter is yellow, and the symbol for the south is the sacred red flowering stick.

"Then, standing in the center of the circle, we raise the pipe and offer it to the sky, sending forth a voice, 'You in the depths of the heavens, an eagle of power, behold!'

"And last of all, we offer the sacred pipe to the earth, saying, 'And you, Mother Earth, the only mother, you who have shown mercy to your children.'"

I have mentioned the numerous songs with which Black Elk interlaced his tellings. Here is one that we learned from him and that no doubt was put together by my father from bits and pieces Black Elk sang at various times. It does express something of the meaning of the sacred hoop:

See how the grasses show their faces,
From the earth tender faces they are lifting,
Happy faces sunward lifting,
Hey-o-ha! Hey-o-ha!

See where the thunder beings waken,
From the west sending voices they are coming.
Grasses hear them and are happy,
Hey-o-ha! Hey-o-ha!

See where the great white giant wakens,
From the north winds of cleansing he is sending.
Strength he brings us as he passes.
Hey-o-ha! Hey-o-ha!

See where the daybreak star is shining,
With a light pure and searching it is shining,
All things silently are watching,
Hey-o-ha! Hey-o-ha!

See where the holy tree is flowering,
From the earth, bright with birdsong it is flowering.
Happy all who live beneath it.
Hey-o-ha! Hey-o-ha!

See where the sacred sun is walking,
In the blue robe of morning he is walking,
With his power greenward walking,
Hey-o-ha! Hey-o-ha!

We have sung that song many times, and it was a favorite of my father's.

Respectfully impressed as I was when I first heard about the sacred hoop, it may have represented no more than a vaguely beautiful idea to me. But now that I am no longer fourteen, I have learned, in the only way such knowledge may be gained, what Black Elk meant when he said "it is not easy to live in this world." As one of many and varied travelers on the black road of worldly difficulties, I am gaining a greater capacity to see, and perhaps more than a little strength to understand, the meaning and the hope that lie within the simple idea of the sacred hoop.

For beautiful and happy and wonderful as this life undoubtedly is, it remains true that it is not easy to live in this world. And where spiritual understanding crosses—overcomes—casts light upon—worldly difficulties, is not that crossing place truly *holy* in that it represents the triumph of the highest and the best that is in us over the worldly or materialistic? The triumph of courage over difficulty, of the spirit over the material?

Also of increasing importance to me is the idea that this hoop of the universe is large enough to hold all living creatures and everything that grows; its kindly and tolerant concept is inclusive, not exclusive. By the simple fact of our *being* we may all walk together along the black road of difficulties, the road of everyday life. By living in harmony with the creative principle that surrounds us and out of which we come (Black Elk called this "living in a sacred manner"), we may also learn to travel the good red road of spiritual understanding. It is a road on which we must learn to walk; it is a *way*, not a destination.

And when I think about the sacred hoop, I remember Black Elk's words: *"You can just look around you and see that it is so!"*

The Vision
Is Completed

Because it was so different from the day-to-day life of Black Elk and the other storytellers and therefore more difficult to explain, and also because both the holy man and Neihardt considered it the heart of the book to be, the telling of Black Elk's vision took many days. My memory of the period is as if we had been taken into a dreamworld. Almost like a myth it seemed, and yet so real. As it gradually unfolded from day to day, the vision dominated my imagination just as it filled the thoughts of Ben and my father, and surely its recording must have presented a challenge to Enid.

At the beginning of the vision, when two men came down on a small cloud to take the boy Black Elk—who lay ill in his tepee as if dead—to see the grandfathers, it seemed as though I too stepped onto that cloud. My imagination gave the two spirit men faces like those of the young men we knew—Leo Looks Twice and Joe Mesteth, for example. When they reached the rainbow tepee high in the sky, where Black Elk was greeted by the six grandfathers, for me those old men in the cloud tepee, the powers of the six directions, took on the faces of the old men I was seeing every day.

When the horses of different colors—blacks for the west, whites for the north, sorrels for the east, and buckskins for the south—appeared from the four quarters, wheeling and galloping across the sky, I could see them in my mind's eye. We too had horses of those colors—though never had I seen groups of horses proceeding in formation as they did in the vision.

In my imagination I accompanied young Black Elk as he mounted the bay horse he was given and went as Eagle Wing Stretches to the center of the earth—with an eagle on his shoulder. The instructions given him by the old men—the men who were "old like hills, old like stars"—were serious to me. I took them to heart just as the boy Black Elk did, for I was not much older than he, and I identified with him. I remember particularly the time Black Elk charged the "blue man" and in driving a spear through him saved his people from drought. For me it was all vivid and exciting—even if its telling was a bit slow.

The sacred red stick that was given to Black Elk and that he was to take back with him and use for the welfare of his people—I recognized that as the source of the flowering tree that should stand in the center of the sacred hoop. The other gifts he was given by the six old men— the bow and arrows and the cup of water for the west, the white goose's wing and the sacred herb for the north, the pipe and the day-break star for the east, as well as the red stick for the south—these all made sense to me. It was plain to what good and helpful use Black Elk could put "those relics," as Ben called them.

I can express my feelings during those days when Black Elk told about his great vision only by saying that I was in awe of it all—what the six grandfathers told Black Elk and what he was told he must do for his people. Some of the profound meaning of the vision that so im-pressed my father would necessarily escape one of my youthful inex-perience, but I did feel the wonder of it all, and to this day I remember with what beauty my imagination painted the scenes the old man described.

From time to time my father, surprised at what he heard, ques-tioned Ben: "Did the old man *really say that?*" Ben assured him, "Yes, he *did.*"

Black Elk finally completed the telling of the vision on May 19. I no-ticed in both my father and Black Elk a sense of relief, for the portion of the interviews most important to the holy man, and to the writer as well, was now finished. The vision was saved for all people. One might say, "After that it was all gravy."

The Story Continues

We were still camping on Standing Bear's property during the daytime; the interviews were held in various places on his land, and our noon meal was prepared over a small campfire by Daybreak Star Woman. Like Indians, we Neihardts never built the large fires for which whites were then famous, or infamous. We cooked over a very small fire, sometimes built in a hole, sometimes on top of the ground if rocks could be found to contain it. There was always the danger of starting a prairie fire, for the grass was dry everywhere, and should our fire get away from us there would have been no way to prevent its spreading.

While I am talking about my prowess at cooking over an outdoor fire, I must tell you that Enid remarked to her diary, "Hilda is the chief cook. Sometimes Hilda is a bit cranky, but most of the time she is all right!" If confession is good for the soul, let this quotation from my sister be one small boost for that part of my being.

Now that the vision was completed, Black Elk began to tell about his youth, and the stories appealed to my romantic notions in a most gripping manner. I had been fascinated by a little book titled *White Indian Boy,* the story of a white boy who was kidnapped by Indians and grew up with them. He so loved that wild, free life that when he returned to the white world he did not feel at home in that more circumscribed environment. As I read his story, I empathized when he longed for his early freedom, and I understood why the white Indian boy decided to return to his Indian family. Their way of life, free from the constraints of civilization, must have been happy, though hard.

When Black Elk told about his first bow, made by his grandfather, and of his first kill of a small bird, I was right there with him in spirit. I too loved to shoot, and at that time I still loved to hunt with my father.

Black Elk frequently referred to earlier times "when the people were still good." It must have been easier to be good when they lived together as close-knit family or extended family groups. Proper behavior must have been made clear to young boys and girls when grandfathers—who had been men for a long time and knew how to be men —taught their grandsons and grandmothers—who had been women for many years and were filled with knowledge of what women should do—taught their granddaughters. No doubt it was less likely that people would behave in ways the group did not approve when uncles and aunts and cousins were nearby and knew nearly everything everyone did.

In today's more impersonal, larger society, it is not so easy for a young person to find the way he or she should go. Today we look first to what the individual wants; when Black Elk was young the people and their best interests were the primary consideration.

Not having outgrown my love of playing, if one ever does, I was intensely interested in the games Black Elk described. I have already mentioned the hoop and spear game that we all enjoyed so much. Another game that appealed to me was one played by boys, called "throwing them off their horses." Riding their ponies bareback, boys would ride up to one another, take hold, and attempt to pull or throw each other off. It was a rough-and-tumble game, and it prepared boys to be warriors. Back home in Missouri my sister Alice and I played a similar game, imitating knights by galloping toward each other with lances and shields. Why we never were hurt, I cannot say.

When Black Elk and his family wintered at Camp (Fort) Robinson, the children made sleds using buffalo ribs covered with stiff hide for runners. This sounded like fun, but I was not in the least impressed by the games the Indian girls played. Girls' games too were geared toward the part they would take in tribal life. For example, there was one game in which the players pushed a small round piece of bone or a small stone along the ground with their noses—a game that would teach them the womanly virtue of patience! Perhaps my attitude has dimmed my memory of just how it was played.

Another game, perhaps also preparation for being a warrior, was throwing mudballs with a strong and resilient stick, probably a branch from a young tree. With much practice a young man could become both powerful and accurate in projecting the ball at the intended victim. The serious nature of this game was revealed when Black Elk told us, "At that time I was training in throwing mudballs."

Ben demonstrated an old-time contest by which the Lakotas showed their endurance. A seed was placed on the hand and lit, to see how much pain a man could tolerate before he would shake it off. Ben did not light the seed on his hand, but I still remember the imaginary pain I felt when I thought about its burning into the skin.

More than once we had a good laugh about something that was said or that happened. I recall an incident we chuckled over, perhaps because of a difference between our culture and that of the Sioux. Black Elk often said that people should live together, or people and animals should live together, as Ben pronounced it, "like relateeves." This tickled us because in our society *relatives* do not always demonstrate loving congeniality. Of course we did not let our Lakota friends see our amusement; our chuckling was done when we were alone in our tepee.

Now that I am thinking about funny happenings, I recall hearing of an incident when a young warrior rode into camp and started to dismount from his pony. Swinging his right leg over his horse's neck, he turned to slide to the ground. But he had not noticed that a two-year-old colt stood next to his mount, and so as he left his own horse he threw his leg over the surprised young colt, which immediately took off at a run, bucking and making loud noises. Of course the young warrior was facing backward, desperately hanging on to the colt's tail! We all laughed till tears ran down our cheeks.

I recall also a story about a man who had great trouble with chapped lips in the wintertime. They were so sore that he tried to keep from laughing, which made his dry lips crack and bleed, and often he stayed away from people to avoid this. Of course his problem was well known, and naughty little boys liked to try to make him laugh. As Ben related the story to us, it was especially graphic to me because Ben's lips also looked a bit chapped. (It's strange how mental pictures help us remember incidents.) Anyway, one day the man with the chapped lips was fishing, and when Black Elk and his friends managed to make him laugh—most reluctantly—it seemed so funny that Black Elk fell into the water.

There were many such stories, another being about a woman bear who fell in love with a man. We laughed as Black Elk told of the man's embarrassment and the ways he tried to ward off the bear's loving advances. Then there was a tale about a man who climbed a tree to get away from a bear. The branch he sat on broke and he fell, landing right on the broad back of the big grizzly. Of course the bear began running, the man held on for all he was worth, and as they entered the village he called out to the astounded villagers, "See! I've caught a bear!"

We enjoyed those tales, so different from our own, and shared many moments of merriment with our friends.

We Hear about
Big Battles

The next days we went to a draw behind the cabin, where Iron Hawk joined Black Elk and Standing Bear for the talks. For a few days the old men told about battles, and my father was elated with their descriptions of the fights, referring to them in a letter as "some startling accounts of the Fetterman Massacre in 1868 up to the Wounded Knee Fight in 1890." Then, in the same letter, he adds: "This is going to be the first absolutely Indian book thus far written. It is all out of the Indian consciousness."

The old men spoke, as one might expect, colloquially and not in literary fashion, and Ben often had a difficult job interpreting. One exciting and touching episode comes to mind when Iron Hawk was telling about his part in the Battle of the Little Bighorn. The talks had been moved back to Black Elk's place, and we were sitting in the pine shade near the cabin. Iron Hawk, who was still a husky, deep-chested, powerful man in spite of his age, was dramatic in the way he related what happened.

Iron Hawk told us that on the day of the battle he was armed with a bow and arrows. Riding up to a soldier, he shot him with an arrow, and the soldier fell from his horse. Iron Hawk realized the man was not dead, so he jumped off his horse and began beating the trooper with his bow. Graphically he showed us how he did it, wielding an imaginary heavy bow and saying "Hownh!" each time he showed how he had struck the wounded man. "Hownh! Hownh! Hownh!" he repeated, all the time powerfully demonstrating just how he had hit the soldier with the bow. Caught up in Iron Hawk's story, I was mesmerized. Daddy later told me that as I watched and listened my eyes grew larger and larger. Then Iron Hawk, looking over and seeing my expression, smiled sweetly and said, "You see, we were all crazy. We were thinking of the women and children hiding up in the hills."

Another interesting sidelight on a big battle that stands out in my memory is a story about two warriors who, right in the middle of the fighting, got hungry. They went into a wooded area, built a fire, and cooked a meal! They were eating happily when Iron Hawk found them and chided them for leaving the battle. This points up the difference between the whites' attitude toward war and that of the Indians: the whites thought of war as a campaign of considerable duration, whereas the Indians emphasized winning battles or skirmishes, after which a feast and celebration would be in order.

Iron Hawk also told about seeing some boys who discovered a soldier hiding in a clump of bushes. The little boys, who had bows but only blunt arrows, shot at the poor fellow, and each time he was struck the soldier would cry "Ow!" I remember admiring those little boys . . . surely they were great warriors in the making.

The Indian women were feared by the soldiers, I understand, almost more than were the men. After a battle the women would come out of hiding and strip the dead soldiers of their clothing and other valuables, and at times they went so far as to mutilate the bodies. One could hardly blame them, for they saw their menfolk being killed and their land and way of life being taken from them.

After the defeat of the Seventh Cavalry at the Little Bighorn, the women were going about their gruesome chores when they came upon a soldier who was not yet dead. When they tried to remove his clothing he got up and fought them, and everyone laughed at the sight of that naked trooper, fighting with two Indian women.

After the Custer battle, the Indians celebrated their victory with feasting and "kill talks." Black Elk and Standing Bear sang some of these kill songs, and one I particularly liked was Standing Bear's favorite:

A charger, he is coming.
I made him come.
When he came, I wiped him out.
He did not like my ways; that is why.

Black Elk, who was only thirteen at the time, told his story about how the Battle of the Little Bighorn began. Women were out digging turnips, and Black Elk and some other boys were swimming in the river when criers gave the alarm that soldiers were about to attack the village. He and the other boys were told to bring in the horses—quite an undertaking in the excitement and fear of the moment.

Then a call was heard and rapidly spread from group to group: "Crazy Horse is coming! Crazy Horse is coming!" What a thrilling picture that evoked in my imagination, and how exciting it must have been at the moment it occurred.

How the Battle of the Little Bighorn progressed is well-known history, and I have told how the news of its exciting (or tragic) end was brought to the white world by Curly, the Crow scout, and by Captain Grant Marsh of the steamer *Far West*. The news of the battle reached newspapers all over the nation on July 4, 1876, just as Independence Day celebrations were to start.

The Horse Dance

The battle stories completed, during the latter part of the day on May 23 Black Elk began telling about the horse dance, which he had previously caused to be reenacted just as he had seen it in his vision when a small boy. The horse dance is a beautiful dramatization of the sacred hoop and the four directions, with elaborately costumed riders mounted on horses of four colors: black for the west, white for the north, sorrel for the east, and buckskin for the south. Beautiful and virtuous young women, chosen because "nothing bad could be said about them," dressed in red and also painted in that sacred color, sang appropriate songs. Imagine such a dramatic performance being presented out on the prairie! It must have been an inspiring spectacle.

Such a dramatization of Black Elk's vision, a holy man had told him, was necessary so he might bring to his people the meaning and power of the vision. The *meaning* of the vision needed to become part of the people's life, and only through such a performance could Black Elk release himself from the obligation placed on him by the grandfathers. I understand that the horse dance, which has considerable dramatic possibilities, has been performed again by Sioux people in recent years. It was also performed in 1967 in Bancroft, Nebraska, by the Bancroft Saddle Club under the direction of Evelyn Vogt, founder of the John G. Neihardt Foundation. Before that time my sister Alice, while employed as a counselor for a girls' camp, produced another well-received rendition of the horse dance, in which she used the song I quoted in the earlier chapter about the sacred hoop.

As usual, Black Elk's telling of the horse dance included many songs. Enid related this in her diary: "It seems that whenever he would sing a certain song, the horses all danced around! I don't blame the horses, for it [the song] certainly was a beauty! I am beginning to really enjoy Indian songs." The songs sung in those times were often melodious, as were many we heard in 1931, and I am told that the reason many such melodies might not be remembered or known today is that they were "private" songs, not made generally available.

After the rubbing out of Custer and his men at the Little Bighorn and the subsequent violent reprisals inflicted on the Plains tribes by the army, Black Elk and many others sought safety in Canada. But Black Elk was not happy there and, homesick, he returned to his plains country and lived, as far as that was still possible, the familiar, old-time life of his tribe.

Black Elk's accounts of buffalo hunts are most exciting. I was particularly taken with the story of one hunt during a great blizzard when some of the hunters, and the buffalo as well, fell into a ravine filled with snow. How the men got out and returned to their village with meat for all was quite a tale.

With the
Wild West Show

Since Black Elk's European travels were such a departure from the traditional life of the Sioux that we had been hearing about, and since I dreamed of foreign travel myself, that part of his life story sparked my imagination. In November 1886 Black Elk, Standing Bear, and many other Sioux joined Buffalo Bill's Wild West Show, going first to Omaha, Nebraska, where they put on a performance. From there they traveled by train to New York City and performed at Madison Square Garden for about three months, then set sail for England. Black Elk described the stormy crossing of the Atlantic as a terrifying experience.

In England the troupe performed at a Jubilee celebration for Queen Victoria: Black Elk recalled that the audience kept crying out "Jubilee! Jubilee!" Black Elk described the queen as a small, chubby woman with soft hands (so unlike those of the Oglala women back home) who told the Indian performers, "You are beautiful people, and if you belonged to me, I would treat you better."

Black Elk and some friends were having such a good time in London that they missed the boat when the Buffalo Bill show left for the Continent. Luckily they chanced upon another show—Mexico Joe's Wild West Show—and were invited to join it. In Paris they found enthusiastic crowds awaiting them, and Black Elk became friendly with a young French girl, who took him to visit her parents. Black Elk did not give us much detail about that relationship, but knowing how attracted the Europeans were (and are) to American Indians, it may well have been quite a romantic interlude in his life.

During his stay with the French family in "Par's," Black Elk became ill, fainted, and dreamed that he returned to his home on the reservation in South Dakota, where everything seemed in turmoil. When he awoke in Paris he was no longer ill, but he was desperately homesick. The manager of the show made arrangements for his return home.

Back on the reservation, things were just as desperate as Black Elk had dreamed, and many Lakotas were becoming interested in the news about the Ghost Dance movement. At first Black Elk did not believe the story that came from the Paiute Wovoka, but he made an effort to learn more, and finally he doubted no longer. He joined in the dancing and had a vision in which he was shown a type of shirt that should be made and painted in a sacred manner and worn during the dance of the ghosts. Such a shirt, many believed, would protect the wearer from bullets. Black Elk helped make those Ghost Dance shirts.

The interviewing must have ended in late afternoon on that day, for there was time for Enid and me to ride to Manderson for the mail. Mail was always of great importance to my father, and a day without mail—a holiday, for instance—left him frustrated. No doubt on this day all three of us hoped for a letter from Mother in Missouri. As devoted as she was, it is quite likely that a letter did arrive, written in her careful, artistic hand.

We had finished another fine day on the reservation, and we looked forward to a trip that Black Elk, Ben, and Daddy had planned for the next day.

We Learn and Visit
at Wounded Knee

On May 24, we arose earlier than usual and drove over to Wounded Knee battlefield. In 1931 the long grave of the slain people was still just a partially healed gash in the earth; the monuments, gravestones, and cyclone fence that surround the site today were not yet there.

We found a good place to camp for the day on top of that historic hill and spread our blankets on the dry grass. Then Black Elk began his story about the tragic massacre that occurred there on December 29, 1890. I remember that we walked all over the hill and down the gulch where the killing happened, and Black Elk told us much of his story as we walked.

For some reason my memory holds a particularly clear picture of the draw down which the Indian women and children, and some unarmed warriors as well, ran in their attempt to escape from the mounted soldiers. That gully seemed to me—it *is*—very small, shallow, and treeless; surely it could have offered little shelter to those frightened people. The fairly flat land on each side must have made it cruelly easy for the men of the Seventh Cavalry to ride along and, as Black Elk said, butcher those poor defenseless humans as they fled. The troopers' instilled notion that they were heathens or savages no doubt made it easier to shoot them down like rabbits.

I was fascinated as Black Elk dramatically showed us how he had ridden in front of the cavalry, daring them to try to shoot him, because he believed his body was bulletproof. When Black Elk rode in front of them, several women and children who were fleeing from the attacking soldiers were able to escape. On that day Black Elk was not hit by the soldiers' fire, but the following day, when he again rode in front of the cavalrymen—without a weapon—holding his sacred stick up before him as he had safely done the day before, in a moment of doubt or fear he dropped the hand in which he held the sacred stick. Because he did this, Black Elk told us, he was struck by a bullet that tore into his abdomen. Pulling up his shirt, he showed us the scar from the wound. Enid's notation for the day in her diary informs us that Black Elk told us he was not killed "because he was sacred to the Great Spirit."

A touching sidelight on the day of the massacre comes from what Black Elk said he found as he rode from Pine Ridge to Wounded Knee. As he approached the hill where the fighting was going on, he saw a dead woman lying on the ground and, still cradled in her arms, a baby that was trying to nurse. Black Elk dismounted, picked up the child, wrapped it in a blanket the dead mother held, and gently placed the bundle in a safe spot he could return to later. Afterward, he took the baby girl to a good woman who was nursing her own child, and she cared for her. I have wondered if Black Elk later became acquainted with that girl. Perhaps he did.

After the dreadful events at Wounded Knee, Black Elk returned to Pine Ridge, where many of his people had gathered. They had not entirely given up hope, and groups of warriors chased the soldiers and fought them. But the people knew, or began to realize, that the old times were gone. They no longer had the power to fight, and since their beloved land had been taken from them, nothing could ever be the same. But life would somehow continue, and on their reservation Black Elk and his people tried to live as nearly as they could in the good old ways. "After that," Black Elk told us simply, "I got married."

In spite of the intensity of the interviews, we always had good times along with the serious work. Enid and I took a bath in Wounded Knee Creek, using sand for soap. "We were really clean when we got through, too," Enid recorded; "then we got out on the bank and dried ourselves off in the sun. It was lots of fun."

For those who shudder at the thought of using sand for bath soap, be assured that the fine sand did the job and was not at all painful. We always used sand to wash our hands if no soap was available, and we found it ever so handy for washing dishes and cooking utensils in

Black Elk stands on the edge of Cuny Table overlooking the Badlands. Here he prayed for the success of Neihardt's book, for the continued welfare of both families, and for the return of their beloved Black Hills to his people (Neihardt Papers).

Top of Harney Peak—the "center of the earth" of Black Elk's vision. When he returned to the scene of his vision in 1931, Black Elk stood on a more easily accessible spot just below the highest part of the peak, as noted by the black mark on the photograph.

Standing Bear's painting of the center of the earth.

The famous photograph Neihardt took of Black Elk as he prayed to the six grand-fathers on Harney Peak. His red underwear modestly represents how his body was painted red during his vision (Neihardt Papers).

We camped all summer in 1934 on Ben Black Elk's land beside Wounded Knee Creek (Neihardt Papers).

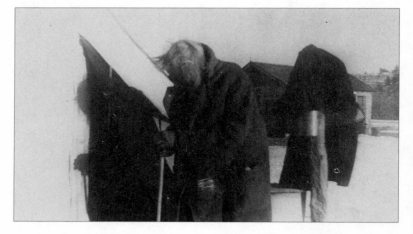

Eagle Elk enters the tent where he lived when Neihardt interviewed him in 1944. His daughter's cabin is in the background. Although she wanted him to live with her, Eagle Elk refused to live in a house (Neihardt Papers).

Eagle Elk had been a handsome young man. Here he is shown in a drawing by Sheila Sanford based on a 1944 photograph taken by Neihardt.

John Neihardt and Black Elk at the Victory Celebration in Pine Ridge, September 14, 1945.

Neihardt's last picture of Black Elk, about 1945.

Ben Black Elk as a performer at Keystone, South Dakota. Picture given to "Kola Hilda" in 1955.

Duhamel's
Sioux Indian Pageant
Program
Rapid City in the Black Hills

Black Elk, Medicine Man of the Pageant

The Old West

The Pageant is one of the few living remnants of the Old West, giving you the history, religion, habits and other characteristics of the Mighty Sioux Nation. Every participant is a full blood Sioux, an old timer who has lived the actual life he is portraying. During each reproduction he actually lives again in heart and soul the days of his forefathers when he was a young person. A reenactment of the old time tribal ceremonies such as the Sun Dance, Love Call, Medicine Dance, Indian Burial, Omaha War Dance, Sioux Songs, etc. **Interesting, Historical, Educational, Glamorous.** The war cry of the last savage mingling with the soft beat of the tom-tom will make your blood tingle.

Two Shows Daily
8:30 a. m. — 8:00 p. m.

Flier for the Duhamel Pageant in the Black Hills. Black Elk performed in the pageant for several years.

John Neihardt gives Black Elk's Prayer on the grounds of the John G. Neihardt Center in Bancroft, Nebraska, at the 1973 Neihardt Day—his last appearance there. Photograph by Elizabeth Jacobs Otradovsky.

Lucy Black Elk Looks Twice outside her home near Manderson, South Dakota. Photograph by Elizabeth Jacobs Otradovsky.

Lucy Black Elk Looks Twice at Stephens College in Columbia, Missouri, April 7, 1977. Photograph by Elizabeth Jacobs Otradovsky.

whatever stream or spring was nearby. Remember that civilization had not yet introduced its various contaminants to that unspoiled land.

After we were dry and dressed, Enid and I went to the store at Brennan to get some bread and milk so we could finish preparing a good meal over the campfire. We ate, and then Black Elk finished telling of the horse dance. I recall how intensely Daddy was affected by the idea of that dance, which he thought could be very effectively depicted in a motion picture. What a scene it would make, with brightly painted Indian riders on many-colored horses, running and circling in symbolic maneuvers, and through it all the ponies neighing to each other.

In relaxing intervals between the recorded interviews, Neihardt often spoke to Black Elk about his own experiences as a writer. Since there was not so much for Black Elk to tell on this day, there was time for an ordinary visit. I remember a conversation they had, perhaps on this day, when my father told Black Elk how he had been able to describe—quite correctly, it was later determined—part of the terrain in *The Song of Hugh Glass*, though he had not previously had a chance to visit the area. This lack was unusual, because Daddy normally made it a point to travel to the locations he would be writing about, and his descriptions were from firsthand observation. Black Elk seemed to take this revelation as a matter of course, though my father thought it rather surprising, and he said Neihardt was what the Indians called "a sacred man thinker."

The relationship between Black Elk and Neihardt was remarkable, and the empathic understanding the holy man had apparently felt on their first meeting increased as the interviews progressed. In a letter to a friend, Daddy described something of the remarkable affinity between himself and Black Elk: "A strange thing happened often while I was talking with Black Elk. Over and over he seemed to be quoting from my poems. Sometimes I quoted from my stuff to him, which when translated into Sioux could not retain much of its literary character, but the old man immediately recognized the ideas as his own. There was very often an uncanny merging of consciousness between the old fellow and myself, and I felt it and remembered it."

After the visiting on the Wounded Knee grounds, we decided we should start for the cabin, because a storm was coming. The storm arrived, with dark clouds, wind, and much flying dust, but no rain. On the way back to Black Elk's home, Enid relates in her diary, Daddy shot a prairie chicken and two quail, which we planned to have for breakfast the next morning.

It was late when we arrived home, but Ellen and Lucy had kept supper warm for us. Satisfied by a good meal, happy over the day's accomplishments, but very weary, we went to bed at once in our tepee. The next day we would go to see Cuny Table in the Badlands.

Cuny Table in
the Badlands

The morning of May 25 was different from other mornings only because we were scurrying around getting ready to go to Cuny Table, in
the Badlands a few miles northwest of Manderson. Black Elk and Ben
owned some land there, and we were eager to see this "table" and the
Stronghold where the Lakotas had gone for safety when they were
overpowered or seriously threatened by an attacking force. Black Elk
had told us about it the day before when he described what he had
seen of the Wounded Knee massacre. For my father it was especially
important that we go there: Cuny Table and the Stronghold would be
important in his *Song of the Messiah,* because that is where Sitanka—
Big Foot—and his band had fled, hoping to meet other friendly Indians, before the army ordered them to go to Wounded Knee in December 1890.

The five of us left at about eight in the morning, driving in our
Gardner. We arrived at the Black Elks' land on Cuny Table about noon
and made camp on a flat place that overlooked the Badlands. In the
distance we could see the Black Hills and Harney Peak. We thought it
a most beautiful spot, and the view out over those godforsaken Badlands, created by countless years of erosion by wind and water, was
like nothing Enid and I had ever seen. In every direction for miles and
miles lay bare, treeless hills, valleys devoid of grass, sharp peaks, and
tall towers; bearing down on it all the bright sun shone, unrelieved by
a single cloud. Not a creature was to be seen, and surely that barren but
compelling terrain would be most inhospitable to any living thing, ani-

mal, plant, or human. Yet, Daddy told us, people *had* crossed it, but at what sacrifice!

Cuny Table was larger than I had expected, a roughly rectangular piece of land fairly flat on top and covered with grasses that were brownish and dry, like all the vegetation that spring. We made our little camp near one edge of the table, right next to the Badlands.

Always careful, Daddy dug a hole in the ground in which we built a fire with sticks and other fuel we found lying around. We cooked some prairie chickens he had killed on the way (my readers will, I fear, get their fill of this western delicacy) and completed our dinner with some crackers (since the little store where we had stopped on the way was out of bread) and coffee with cream. After we had eaten with the relish born of outdoor activities, Black Elk continued with the story of his life.

Later in the afternoon, just before we left, Black Elk stood on the edge near the falling-off place where Cuny Table dropped precipitously into the Badlands, offered his pipe to the sky above, and prayed to the six grandfathers of his vision. He prayed that the powers might help "my friend Mr. Neihardt" make a success of the book he would write, that both our families would be well, and that we might all be together again in the near future. But above all, he prayed that the land taken from his people so many years before might someday be returned to them. That was always his fervent prayer.

Enid was appropriately impressed, as were we all, and commented later to her diary: "It was a beautiful prayer, all right. And Black Elk made it up right on the spot, too, which made it all the more wonderful. This was the most sincere prayer."

The way leading to the top of Cuny Table at that time could hardly be called a road, for it was exceedingly steep, rough, and full of ruts washed by rains. We had managed to crawl up it, the Gardner straining in low gear, winding our way from one side of the narrow road to the other to find the most negotiable route. Although Enid frequently drove on our trip, Daddy had taken over the wheel as we neared the precarious approach to the table. The path was very high in the center, and while we were driving back down, the drain plug on our crankcase was knocked off. Ben, always creatively handy, found a way to plug the drain and stop the leaking for a time, so that we were able to drive back home without ruining the engine. This was indeed fortunate, for it was almost dark, and the thought of being caught out in the Badlands at night was not appealing.

It was twilight as we drove back to Manderson, and on the way "Deadeye Dick" Neihardt bagged three more prairie chickens. One of them, hard to see in the dim light, was only wounded and ran around after being hit. Daddy, Ben, and I chased it and soon put it out of its misery. Afterward Ben cheerily pointed out, "We had a Chase-in-the-*Evening*, didn't we?" Of course Enid and I found this play on our fine friend's name very funny, and we joined in as Ben chuckled, "Huh-huh-huh!"

My father worried about the propriety of his hunting on the reservation and often asked Ben about it. Ben responded with emphasis, "This is *our* land, and we can hunt whenever we want to." Often when we hunted, Ben would sit on one front fender and I on the other as Daddy or Enid drove along slowly. From this vantage we could better spot a prairie chicken or pheasant and point it out to our marksman.

On the way home we stopped at a store for some provisions, and when we arrived at the cabin we found Ellen and Lucy awaiting our return. As we entered, Ben handed Ellen a sack, saying imperiously, "Wimmens, here's some eggs. Cook 'em! We're hungry!" Enid, a real man's woman, laughed at this male witticism. But I, perhaps already showing symptoms of a frame of mind that in later years would be termed feminist, must have revealed by my expression that I did *not* think it funny for him to issue such peremptory orders to our two good friends, our fellow women. Ben saw this, understood, and looking directly at me, softened the effect by . . .*giggling!* It all worked out well: Ellen and Lucy seemed unperturbed by Ben's joking command; at least they retained their usual modest demeanor. The eggs were cooked, and Ellen made a big batch of her very good biscuits, with which we had something rare—real butter.

On a previous day when we were in the cabin, sitting and chatting while Lucy and Ellen prepared a meal, Black Elk came in and spoke to Ben in Lakota. Since Ben immediately repeated to Ellen what his father had said, it seemed obvious that Black Elk's message was intended for his daughter-in-law. I was confused, and it must have shown on my face, for Ben, always sensitive, explained: "The old man has too much respect for Ellen to speak directly to her. So he tells me what he wants to say, and I tell Ellen." This occurrence provided an interesting peek into a custom that evolved as a response to extended families' living together in a small space, often in one tepee.

After our supper we all sat around the table and visited for a while. Because we had heard so much about vision quests and how boys' or men's names were often taken from some important communication or occurrence in their visions, I naturally wanted to know how girls received their names. This evening I inquired about that. Ben explained: "Girls usually were given a name based on the first thing the mother saw after they were born. So a girl might be called 'Sees White Cow' or 'Brings White Horses.'" For me this was disappointing; surely it was not as appealing or exciting as the men's way of acquiring their names through a vision. But *I* had a name from Black Elk's vision—Daybreak Star Woman. I felt good about that.

It had been a perfect day, and the evening also seemed special. Up there on Cuny Table when Black Elk prayed for our two families and for the success of the interviews, I felt that a quiet and loving bond enveloped the five of us, a closeness of spirit I believe we all shared. It was a warm and happy evening we were having together in Black Elk's cabin.

Now the talk turned to something Black Elk had mentioned several times before, and this evening he brought it up again. He told my father that he would soon be "under the grass" and that before he died he wanted to go again to the center of the earth where he had been taken in his vision. Once more Daddy promised him, "We will go, Black Elk. We will all drive to Harney Peak in the Black Hills together just as soon as your story is finished."

On that happy note we three weary Neihardts retired to blankets in our tepee, and the Black Elks to the iron beds in their cabin.

Gifts Are Given

May 26 was Mother's birthday, and we had not yet let her know we remembered. We rose early, had a good breakfast with the Black Elk family, then went out to the pine shelter and resumed the talks with Black Elk and Standing Bear. It was a time for teaching by the holy man and his friend, and for miscellaneous questions.

Both Black Elk and Standing Bear had often referred to the way their land, particularly the sacred Black Hills, had been taken from them. It was probably on a day like this, when a question would not interrupt a tale that needed finishing, that my father asked about Red Cloud and the Black Hills. When treaty discussions were under way in the 1870s concerning the whites' desire to purchase the Hills, Chief Red Cloud is reported to have said he would "lease" them for seven generations. My father asked what Red Cloud had meant by saying he would lease the Hills.

Black Elk responded that Red Cloud meant that in return for a payment to the Sioux, whites could use the land for seven generations beginning with Red Cloud's son, after which, Black Elk said, "we would still own the land. Then we could decide what to do with it."

Although, as many know, a lawsuit brought to regain their land more than a century ago was concluded in recent years with a substantial money judgment for the Sioux, they continue to demand no less than the return of their beloved Black Hills. How the controversy will turn out remains to be seen.

We talked of many other matters, and I recall that my father, who had considerable interest in psychic research, had asked Black Elk more than once about the Yuwipi ceremony. It is likely that it was also discussed on this day. Whenever he told us about it, the picture of Yuwipi as Black Elk described it remains vivid in my mind.

The Yuwipi happening was held in a large tepee or building. The holy man who was to perform the ceremony was wrapped in a blanket or buffalo robe, then bound with leather thongs and placed on the ground or floor. I seem to recall hearing, though I cannot be sure, that the leather thongs were dampened so the knots would be more difficult to loosen. After the holy man was ready, the place was made dark. Soon balls of light would be seen emanating from the place where the holy man lay and flashing throughout the enclosure. Drumbeats and voices would be heard, as well as messages for those assembled.

After it was over and the lights were on again, the holy man would be found lying on the blanket that had enveloped him, with the leather thongs all loosened.

The description was graphic and exciting, and I remember how impressed I was that the holy man could get loose after he had been tightly bound. How I wished we might see such a ceremony!

Black Elk told us he had participated in Yuwipi many times when he was younger. When my father asked if he would be willing to put on such a ceremony for us, however, Black Elk responded simply but definitely, "I do not care to do that anymore." The impression I had at the time, which I think is correct, is that Black Elk felt he had progressed spiritually far beyond that point. He was no longer interested in such things.

After a morning of miscellaneous discussion and teaching by Black Elk and Standing Bear, we enjoyed a meal that Lucy and Ellen brought out to us in the sunshade. The three weeks available for the interviews were nearly over, and those good women wanted to make sure the talks were not unnecessarily interrupted. After eating, we decided to move over to what Black Elk called the sacred bluff for the rest of the day's interviewing.

The sacred bluff was a high point near Black Elk's home, and we understood that he went there often to "send up a voice" in prayer. Black Elk prayed often while we were with him, wherever we happened to be, and usually he asked that his people might get back into the sacred hoop ("Oh, make my people live!"), that his family and Mr. Neihardt's might prosper, and that his people's land might be restored to them. He never prayed for material things.

On the very top of the sacred bluff and near its edge, a hole had been dug to accommodate the suppliant on a vision quest. Black Elk showed my father how the fasting young man stood in the depression, which was about two or three feet deep, and prayed to the four quarters, the sky, and the earth for a vision that would show what he was to do in his life and by what name he would be called. The hole had been roughly dug, and all around its edges grew dry buffalo grass and weeds. I remember wondering vaguely about rattlesnakes, but this thought did not deter Ben and my father, who stepped down into the hole and posed for a snapshot.

The view from the sacred bluff was especially beautiful. Without the sparse vegetation, it would have been as awe inspiring as the views in the Badlands, as Enid pointed out in her diary.

While we were all sitting on the bluff, quietly gazing out across the strange land we had come to love, Black Elk made us know, in his special quiet but meaningful way, that he wanted to make an announcement. We were eager to hear what he would say, and after a pause he revealed what was on his mind. Since the interviewing would soon be over, there was something he wanted to do.

Simply, but with his usual great dignity, the old holy man took in his right hand the pipe he had used throughout the interviews. Then he held it out to Neihardt, saying that he wanted my father to have it and keep it always with him. Then, after a long pause, he stated that he had now given his power to my father and that he was left just a poor old man.

Black Elk told the deeply moved poet that he was also going to entrust "my nephew" with the cup of water for the west, the white goose's wing for the north, and the sacred hoop of the people and the staff he had used in so many ceremonies, which represented the south. The daybreak star ornament, representing the east, he had given my father the year before, and today he had given the pipe, which also is a symbol for the east. "When you leave us, you must take them with you," he said.

Just what my father told Black Elk then I cannot say, but I am sure he spoke well and with appreciation. I also feel sure no words would have been necessary. Truly each man knew what the other felt in his heart.

Later in the afternoon Enid and I suggested it might be fun to go swimming, and the men agreed. But a trip to the pool on Wounded Knee Creek convinced us the water was still too cold, so we left that inviting patch of water. It would be ready later on for a fine swim—even though we were not there to enjoy it.

Back at Black Elk's home, we learned that Ellen needed some supplies before she could cook supper. Enid and I got in Ben's old Ford and drove to Manderson for the items she requested. After supper we had a rabbit dance, and Enid and I acted as starters. Enid had been learning social dancing at home, so she guided me playfully in a fox-trot to the two-beat rabbit dance music. Ben looked shocked, interrupted our demonstration, and showed us the *right* way to dance the rabbit! We all laughed, then Enid and I carefully danced the right way. A bit later we all realized we were tired, so we said a fond good-night to our hosts, and everyone went to bed.

On May 27, we finally got Mother's birthday present ready. Daddy had purchased a couple of pieces of Indian beadwork that we thought were very pretty. Enid wrapped them nicely with whatever paper was available at the trading post, and the parcel was ready to be mailed the next day.

We Learn More, but
the End Is in Sight

That evening Lucy prepared supper for just the three of us. Everyone else was gone; perhaps they had an emergency or a special celebration at Ben's house. This was one time we had trouble eating everything that was offered. Lucy put some chokecherry sauce on the table, and, though we each tried to eat some, we just didn't like it. What should we do, not to offend Lucy? My suggestion was followed: we all took a little on our plates and pushed it around, hoping she would think we actually had eaten some. While we were still eating, Ben came home, noted that the bowl of chokecherry sauce was nearly full, and asked, "Did you put any sugar on the sauce?" When we said no he remarked, "Well, I don't see how you ever ate it, then!" So we tried some with sugar. It was edible, but not really what we considered good, even *with* sugar.

We had another rabbit dance that evening, with none other than the great Black Elk as drummer and singer. This time Enid and I danced carefully: two steps forward and one back, two steps forward and one back, around and around in a circle. Daddy, of course, did not join in the dancing, but we all had fun.

Another wonderful day had passed, and we were ready for bed. Following our usual procedure of checking the ground in our tepee for intruders, we threw our blankets down and were soon fast asleep on Mother Earth.

On May 28 we were alone with Ben and "the old man," for all the others in the family had gone to the Indian council at the mission. I especially remember that day, for it was the only time the whole family was away. When I asked where Lucy and Ellen and the others were, the response from Ben or my father—I do not recall which one answered my question—left me with the sense that their absence was something of a secret and not to be mentioned. So deeply were we all caught up in the mystique of Black Elk's narrations that their attendance at the council seemed almost disloyal. That vague feeling persists today.

Since the "wimmens" were away, our dad cooked the noon dinner. He made old-fashioned dumplings, steamed in a large pot over a prairie chicken he had stewed. Daddy was really a good cook, though we children thought he got a little too creative when he occasionally prepared meals at home when Mother was not well. This time Enid and I found the dumplings quite acceptable. Ben had never eaten dumplings before, thought them delicious, and more than once afterward recalled how good they were, shaking his head, smiling, and saying, "Oh, them dumplin's!"

After the noon dinner Black Elk completed the telling of his life, and conversation became more general. Perhaps the fact that others in the family had gone to the Catholic mission prompted my father to ask Black Elk a question that must often have occurred to him. He asked why Black Elk, whose story revealed beliefs of such beauty and spiritual meaning, was a member of a white church. Black Elk thought for a moment or two, then he replied quite simply, "Because my children have to live in this world." I could never forget those words.

Previously we had been told about something that happened when he was young and just beginning to use his powers to cure illness. The youthful medicine man was praying for the sick person's recovery and using his rattle as part of a healing ceremony when a priest burst into the tepee, grabbed young Black Elk and pulled him rudely outside. Then he took Black Elk's sacred rattle, threw it to the ground, and stamped on it, admonishing the surprised young man that he should never use such "heathen" objects again.

I was deeply troubled by this story, for the atmosphere of our interviews was permeated with respect for Black Elk, and we held his spiritual power in high regard. More than once since learning about the episode, I have wondered what real difference there could possibly be between a Sioux holy man's shaking his rattle up and down and a priest's swinging his golden censer back and forth.

Black Elk told my father that later he did join the white church, and we knew he catechized young children. What he did not find it necessary to say left us with a strong sense of where his true beliefs remained. Understanding all too well, Neihardt said no more.

Leaving that sensitive, vaguely unpleasant subject, we turned eagerly to plans for our trip to Harney Peak the next day. At long last Black Elk's often-expressed desire to return to the place where he had been taken in his great vision was going to become reality. Black Elk had told my father he had something to say to the six grandfathers while he stood on Harney Peak, and we were eager to learn what that might be.

The next day the five of us would leave in our Gardner and Ben's old Ford for Sylvan Lake, and from there we would climb Harney Peak. Both cars were needed because after our trip up the mountain we would leave our friends, they to return to Manderson and we to Branson, Missouri. It was a sad thought, and we did not dwell on it, for our biggest adventure still lay ahead.

That evening we packed all our belongings and put them in the Gardner. In the morning we would take down the tepee, for it would go home with us.

The Vision
Revisited

Early the next morning—it was May 29, 1931—we completed our packing, dismantled our beloved tepee, and put everything not loaded the evening before into the backseat of the Gardner. Ben and Black Elk put their belongings into Ben's Ford, and our little caravan started on the long-awaited drive to Harney Peak.

We were happy to be on our way for the anticipated adventure but sad that we must say good-bye to Lucy, Ellen, and Leo, who had been so good to us. I would not see Lucy or Ellen again for many years. As for Leo Looks Twice—Leo, who had so often gruffly invited me to go out on horseback: "Hilda, do you want to ride-out?"—Leo I was never to see again. But we did not know that then.

I can imagine, though he did not show it, that Black Elk was even more excited about our trip than we three Neihardts. He considered this his second trip to the center of the earth, the first having been when as a nine-year-old he was taken there in his great vision. We too believed it was so.

We drove to Brennan, then followed dusty Highway 18 to Hot Springs, where we took Highway 83 north through Custer, South Dakota, to Sylvan Lake. I believe it must have been at Hot Springs that we stopped for lunch, and then we found something exciting and novel to do. There was a carnival in town, and Enid and I were eager to go on the Ferris wheel. I remember with what humorous camaraderie the old holy man himself was urged to take a ride on the wheel.

The only thing about this incident that has remained bright and clear in my mind is that Black Elk did ride the Ferris wheel, and that he was terrified. Each time the wheel was stopped to let someone step down or take a seat, it seemed that Black Elk and I were at the very top, rocking precariously back and forth. That was a bit disconcerting even for someone who had ridden a wheel before, but for Black Elk it was worse. I don't know whether Ben had ever ridden a Ferris wheel, but certainly Black Elk had not. Each time the wheel turned so our seats were near the ground and it would have been possible to let us off, Black Elk called out: *"'top! 'top!"* That was the only English word I ever heard him say. Of course our ride did finally end, and the Ferris wheel did (s)top.

The carnival was not the only entertainment in town that day. There was a motion picture theater, so Daddy took us all to see a show. I do not recall what picture was playing, but one character was a beautiful young woman who behaved in a way Black Elk thought improper. Perhaps she was brazen or forward or flirty. I was sitting beside him in the darkened theater, and each time the actress did something a good young woman should not do, Black Elk said, *"Sheetsha! Sheetsha!"* (Bad! Bad!) I wonder what he would think about a modern movie? No doubt the one we saw in 1931 would seem modest today.

The road to Sylvan Lake at the base of Harney Peak was a scenic but dusty, winding way through pines and the rocky beginnings of the mountains. It was a most fitting overture for the great event that was to come, and our anticipation was immense. We arrived there late in the afternoon, and my dad rented two cabins—one for Black Elk and Ben and one for the three Neihardts. We were very happy that evening, for the interviews had gone much better than could have been anticipated, and the mass of wonderful new material he had collected must have made my father impatient to get home and begin work on the book. Yes, he was a happy man that evening. We all were happy, yet not without a hint of sadness around the edges of our joy.

In those days, whenever we were camping, whether in a cabin or in a tent or tepee, we had a great time, for our dad combined an intensely serious nature with a fun-loving side. He joked a lot. I do not wish to idealize him, for he was certainly a very human person with human shortcomings, but still I cannot recall a time when he was impatient with us children, even when we were very young. He treated us like good friends, and we responded that way, our attitudes colored by our great respect for the person he was.

During the late afternoon the five of us walked along the shore of Sylvan Lake, taking in the beauty of it all—the clear lake, the tall pines, and the severe rocky peaks that were so close. As we strolled beside the lake, I was taken with a great desire to go swimming. I did not notice the look on Ben's or my father's face when I announced what I wanted to do. Hastily donning a swimsuit, I dived from a rock on shore into the deep, clear water. Then I heard laughter coming from the bank as I found out the water was *much* too cold for a swim! It was, in fact, downright icy. I turned the minute my head came out of the water and swam quickly for shore. We had more than once gone swimming in the Missouri Ozarks in the middle of winter, just on a dare, but this time the chill was unexpected. When I reached the shore and climbed out, I hurried to the cabin to change. Then, dry and warming, I joined in the general laughter. I had learned that late May is not the beginning of the swimming season in the Black Hills.

On the morning of May 30 the five of us breakfasted at Sylvan Lodge, then started the long walk to the top of the rocky peak called Harney. Isn't it ironic that the peak bears the name of an army general who was no friend to the Indians? The path up the mountain is said to be four miles, but what a long four miles it is! One would not call it true mountain climbing, but it surely is very heavy hiking.

The problem I have noticed, in my several climbs in recent years, is that the path goes up for a while, then down, so you feel dismayed at losing altitude you had already gained and must now retake. The altitude at Sylvan Lake is approximately 6,000 feet, and the top of Harney Peak is 7,240.

On that morning the climb seemed fairly easy to the three of us, for we often hiked in the rugged Missouri Ozarks. For Ben too the hike was not demanding, but for Black Elk, who at sixty-eight seemed exceedingly old to me, it was not so easy, and we did stop several times for him to rest. I remember feeling like a puppy, running back and forth as we climbed, drinking in all the wonders of the mountains. On the way up we looked across from one rocky promontory to another and saw a white mountain goat basking in the sunshine.

During the climb up the peak, Ben told us that Black Elk had re-marked to him, in his mysterious way, that if he still had power, some-thing should happen up on the mountaintop. When Ben asked what that might be, he had responded that there should be "a little light-ning, a little thunder, and a little rain." Since his power had come from the west, from the thunder beings, such would be the greeting they would send him. *If* he still had power.

Today there is a small concrete building on top of the peak that is no longer used for its original purpose as a forester's lookout. The upper part of Harney has recently been designated by Congress as "Black Elk Wilderness," thanks to a bill promoted by Senator George McGovern of South Dakota. But in 1931 it was still in its pristine state. I recall no stairs like those that now exist just before you reach the top, and I do not remember how we negotiated that last rocky, precipitous part. No doubt we just *climbed,* and it did not seem remarkable to us then.

When we reached the partially flat, rocky summit, we were inspired by the view in all directions, made more impressive by the blue haze that clung above the horizon. I remember clambering about, explor-ing the rocky surface of the peak and stopping, breathless, before the sudden drop-offs.

So historic has the event become that happened on top of Harney Peak that I almost hesitate to describe it. I shall tell it as it seemed to me then and let the reader fill in the aura with which the years have clothed that moment.

Black Elk had carefully planned what would happen on the peak. Before leaving Manderson, he had purchased a set of red flannel un-derwear. In his vision his whole body had been painted red, and to re-enact the scene on this day, he really should have been naked, his body painted red, wearing only a breechclout. But Enid and I were there and he did not wish to embarrass us. Thus the red underwear.

Black Elk went behind a large rock, and after a few minutes he came out wearing the red underwear with a breechclout over it. Then, with his sacred pipe, he was ready to stand on the highest part of the rocky peak and send forth a voice to the six grandfathers of the universe.

Looking about the rough surface of the peak, Black Elk immediately recognized and pointed out to my father the particular high, jutting rock on which he had stood in his vision. Because that point was not easily reached, however, Black Elk chose a lower portion of rock that was as near as possible to the sacred spot. Now he stood on that flat rock, offering the pipe with its mouthpiece upward in one hand and reaching skyward with the other.

As the holy man sent forth his voice to Wakan Tanka, the Great Mysterious, offering the stem of his pipe to the One Above, my father took the picture of Black Elk that more than one photographer has praised. The camera he used was a Kodak 3A, with a pull-out bellows for focusing, and it took a postcard-sized picture. Black Elk holds the pipe in his left hand, with his right hand uplifted, palm forward to the emptiness in front of him. I mention this because Black Elk had stated more than once that the pipe should always be held in the right hand. Was there a sacred reason he held it differently on that day?

It was chilly on top of the mountain, and Enid caught a cold, both because of the unaccustomed altitude and because she had not removed her jacket as we climbed. In spite of the chill in the air, we four stood silent and transfixed behind Black Elk as he prayed. Looking back to that moment, I find it hard to believe I was there. But I was. Ben, John Neihardt, Enid, and I—we were all there. And we watched and listened.

Looking up into the bright, brassy, cloudless sky, the holy man faced the west, whence his power came, held his pipe with its buffalo-hide-covered mouthpiece toward the sky, reached up and out with his other hand, and spoke words that have touched the hearts of many. Let me recall some of those words:

Tunkashila, Wakan Tanka [Grandfather, Great Mysterious], you have been always, and before you nothing has been. . . . There is nothing to pray to but you. You yourself, everything that you see, everything has been made by you. The four quarters of the earth you have finished; the day, and in that day, everything you have finished.

Grandfather, lean close to the earth, that you may hear the voice I send.

Grandfather, Great Mysterious, all over the world the faces of living things are alike. In tenderness they have come up out of the ground. Look upon your children, with children in their arms, that they may face the winds and walk the good road to the day of quiet.

In sending up my voice I pray that you may cause the tree to bloom again so that my people may see happy days. My grandfathers, you have sent me to the center of the earth and showed me the good things that were to be. Hear me now, that my people may live.

Again, and probably for the last time, I recall my vision and call upon you for help. I send a voice again so that you may hear me and bring my people back into the sacred hoop. At the center of the hoop there should be a tree, a tree that was to bloom and help us.

Hear me, O Great Mysterious One, that my people may live and that the tree may bloom, and that the people may see happy days and the happy land that you have promised.

Tunkashila, Grandfather, behold this pipe. In behalf of my children and also my nephew's children, I offer this pipe, that we may see happy days!

As Black Elk prayed, a little black cloud had come overhead, and a scant, cool rain began to fall. As the drops of rain mingled with the tears running down his face, the holy man cried out: "Oh, make my people live!"

The little black cloud went back the way it had come, and the rain stopped.

It Was All Over

The descent from Harney Peak was less strenuous than the morning's climb, though it was uphill part of the way. We were quiet as we walked, each with our own thoughts. What Black Elk had said up there on the strange, rocky mountaintop, and the soft rain that had fallen just as he said it should, had made a strong impression on us all. The whole experience of the day—the little black cloud, the distant thunder, the lightning, and the scant rain, coming when rain was so unexpected—did seem fraught with mystery. How could it have been other than an acknowledgment to Black Elk from the six grandfathers?

We were all very hungry when we reached our cabins near Sylvan Lake, and Daddy thought we should have dinner together at the lodge. But when we got there we found no meals were being served, that only lunches were available. Daddy bought ten roast beef sandwiches, and we returned to the cabins to eat.

I recall only the subdued mood of the evening. We were happy, dear friends eating together, but all of us were enveloped in the feeling that we had been in the presence of something very large, very mystical, very meaningful.

It was so. Through the succeeding years, that feeling of mystery was to remain with us all and to grow in power. To me, it was to be an inspiration for my life.

The next morning—June 1—we again packed our belongings into the two cars and drove to Hill City, where Daddy filled Ben's Ford with gas and oil. Then we went our separate ways, Ben and Black Elk returning to Manderson while we started for home. The way we felt then is well expressed by Enid's simple entry in her diary: "We told them good-bye and sadly parted."

We did not head directly for our home in Missouri, for Daddy wanted to show us something of his beloved Black Hills. From Hill City we drove to Deadwood, South Dakota, where we stayed in the Rainbow Tourist Camp and visited the saloon in which Wild Bill Hickok, a book hero of mine at the time, was shot in the back. After looking around that historic town, we drove the next morning to the town of Spearfish on Little Spearfish Creek, where Daddy and his mother and sisters had spent the summer in 1907.

The little railroad that went up through the canyon and had been considered a modern engineering miracle was still there. Dad told us about the good times he and his family had that summer—about the abandoned town they came upon in their wanderings, whose inhabitants had simply left, leaving behind most of their furniture and other belongings. He told us how he and his sisters rode on the narrow-gauge railroad, still intact from mining days. Behind the door of a barbershop, he had found an old buffalo gun with German silver fittings. Years later the gun was badly broken in a wreck, and he had the silver fittings mounted on a Savage bolt-action deer rifle for me. The gun was at home in Branson.

Unfortunately, in Spearfish we discovered that the rear end of the Gardner had gone out, and we were delayed for repairs. Parts had to be ordered from Denver, and as one might expect, they were slow in coming. We stayed in a cabin camp at Spearfish, and Daddy let Mother know about the delay, no doubt by a wire. Without a car, there was not much we could do except hike among the beautiful mountains that are the backdrop for the town of Spearfish.

When the Gardner was finally repaired and ready for the return trip, we lost no time getting under way, and Daddy and Enid drove long hours to get us home as soon as possible. One night, driving very late and finding no cabin camp when we needed one, we tried to sleep—all three of us—in the car, Daddy in the front and Enid and I in the rear, sharing space with all our baggage and equipment. None of us could sleep, and our attempts were ended by Dad's announcement, "My toes are curling!" After that we drove on, still finding no camp open on the way.

We arrived in Branson after about two days and nights on the road, tired and dusty but happy. It was so good to get home!

A Book
Becomes Reality

I am sure the welcome we received from our mother and grand-mother, and from Sigurd and Alice as well, was as enthusiastic as the welcome we all had given when Daddy and Sigurd returned from their first meeting with Black Elk. After plenty of welcome-home hugs all around, we unloaded the tepee and our other paraphernalia, gave Mother the set of Sioux pottery Daddy had bought for her on the reservation, and let everyone know as well as we could how enjoyable and successful our trip had been. But how could we make them realize what that experience meant to us? Perhaps it would be impossible, but we tried.

Within a day or so, Enid began the work of transcribing her voluminous shorthand notes of the interviews, and Daddy began to plan how the book would be written. Of course he wrote immediately to William Morrow, who had contracted for the book and given the advance that made our trip possible. A response from Morrow and Company brought the disappointing news that Mr. Morrow had died. Although the firm would go ahead with its contract to publish, the editor who would be working with my father did not have Morrow's vision.

The book was written with a speed most unusual for Neihardt. He set aside the manuscript he had been working on—*The Song of the Messiah*—and immediately began the Black Elk story. Everything about the talks and our experience was fresh in his mind, and his enthusiasm for Black Elk and for the mass of new material the interviews had provided gave strong impetus to his writing. So it was that Neihardt began what he had told a friend would be "the first absolutely Indian book thus far written." What he envisioned for the book in that letter would come to pass. The book he would write could be "all out of the Indian consciousness" because its writer, himself so thoroughly and sympathetically in tune with his subject, would introduce nothing that might dilute its true character.

After the manuscript had been submitted to Morrow and Company, a letter from an editor suggested that the vision sequence be placed in an appendix. Rarely had I seen my father so angry, so upset. In discussing that preposterous idea with Mother, he stormed about the house, stating in no uncertain terms that if *that* was the way the publishers felt, he would ask them to return the manuscript, for to him the great vision was the spiritual heart of the entire book. Mother, always wise and supportive, counseled him, "Oh, John, just you wait and see; they'll publish the book exactly as you wrote it!" And of course they did.

I remember my parents' discussions concerning a title. Daddy had considered "The Story of a Holy Man of the Sioux" and several other possible titles. One day in our living room they were talking about what the book should be called, and my mother said, "Oh, John, why don't you just call it *Black—Elk—Speaks?*" She emphasized each word, and my father immediately accepted her suggestion. *Black Elk Speaks* it would be.

It was a good title, but through the years it has, I believe, encouraged more than a little misunderstanding about the authorship of the book. Although a book could hardly have been written that would more faithfully present what Black Elk wanted to say—which he himself could not have done—still it is a work of art, and its author was John Neihardt. The title, whether well chosen or not, does make it clear just how eager Neihardt was to give full credit to Black Elk.

While on the reservation, my father had arranged for Standing Bear to make a series of paintings that would illustrate Black Elk's vision, and a price for each one was suggested by the artist and agreed to by Neihardt. After we were back home the paintings began coming— a few at a time—and Daddy paid for them as they were received.

The paintings were included in the beautiful cloth-bound book

Morrow and Company published in 1932. One immediately notes that the illustration "Black Elk at the Center of the Earth" is remarkably similar to the picture we took of the outcropping of rock where Black Elk had stood in his vision. I do not know whether Standing Bear actually went to Harney Peak before he made the painting or whether the description Black Elk gave while recounting his vision was so clear that the artist could reproduce it in such a striking manner. However that may be, the painting does portray the reality, and all of Standing Bear's paintings have been widely used in publications over the years.

Black Elk Speaks was well received by reviewers and by some readers, though it was given little publicity. Reviewers called it a "beautiful" and "spiritual" book, but the book-reading public of that time was not much interested in the Indian mystique. I suspect that in the thirties most people in this country still viewed as savages and heathens the good folks now respectfully referred to as Native Americans.

Black Elk Speaks was soon out of print, and unsold volumes were remaindered at forty-five cents a copy. Its author could not afford to buy many even at this low price.

Some people did appreciate the message of the book, and among them was the famous Swiss psychiatrist-philosopher Carl Jung. Just how he obtained a copy I do not know, but I have heard that he came upon it while on an American lecture tour. He was impressed, for Black Elk's story provided an excellent illustration of the archetypes he considered so important. In Zurich he prevailed on Walter Verlag, a Swiss publisher, to have the book translated into German.

Although the firm had allowed the book to go out of print more than twenty years before, Morrow and Company asserted a publisher's right to contract for the foreign edition, and my father's request that he be allowed to review the translation was refused. No doubt he would have liked for Mother, who had spoken German from childhood and whose schooling had been mostly in Germany, to read the manuscript before it was published. The translation is in general satisfactory, I assume, but the translator did not correctly render in German the name Black Elk, which is used as the title of the German-language edition, *Schwarzer Hirsch*. *Hirsch* is a deer, and so the Sioux holy man is known in Germany as "Black Deer."

The German-language edition was published in 1955 and seems to be highly regarded. In 1956 my father asked Morrow to return the rights in the book to him. This was done, but the publisher asked him to repay part of the advance made to him in 1931! Using all royalties earned during the brief time the book was in print in this country, and also applying to Morrow's advance all royalties from the German edition, a small sum still remained unearned, and they wanted to be reimbursed. Neihardt sent his check.

The book, today well known and now translated into several foreign languages, was out of print except for the German edition until the University of Nebraska Press gave it new life in a paperback edition in 1961. It was then that the young people of this country, who were searching for spiritual reality, read the book and made it what has been called the young people's Bible.

A talented interviewer on national television was interested in the book and its author, for Dick Cavett was also from Nebraska. In 1971, after making arrangements with Neihardt to appear on his show, Mr. Cavett brought his American Broadcasting Company television crew from New York to Omaha for the interview. The rapport between the dynamic ninety-year-old poet and the equally dynamic young television star was striking. The show was aired nationally in 1971 and repeated in 1972, and a videotape has been shown several times on public television in Nebraska.

Black Elk Speaks was sold successfully in paperback for a number of years by another New York firm, Simon and Schuster, which naturally required exclusive paperback rights. In 1979 a deluxe cloth-bound edition was issued by the University of Nebraska Press. That beautiful book featured an introduction by Vine DeLoria Jr., which is much appreciated by our family and is no doubt one of the finest and most truly understanding critiques yet written on *Black Elk Speaks*. My father died in 1973 at my home near Columbia, Missouri, and in 1987 our family, motivated by a sense of loyalty, returned publishing rights in the book to the University of Nebraska Press.

The popularity of *Black Elk Speaks* continues, and recently the book has been described in an advertisement as "the first and most important testament to the dignity and spirituality of the Native Americans." But perhaps most important is the simple truth that the wish Black Elk expressed to my father in 1931 has been granted: the great vision and his teachings have been preserved "for all people." Those for whom the vision was preserved are grateful that the old holy man told it to someone who understood.

At Home Again in Branson
and Our Return to
Wounded Knee

Our closeness to the Black Elk family did not end with those good-byes at Hill City, South Dakota. The mystique of our experience during those few weeks at Black Elk's home was strong on our return trip. It had been a happy time even though the purpose was serious and the hours of interviewing were long and arduous.

While on the reservation, we had become attached to the land there, so different from the Ozark Mountain country where we lived, and Daddy had talked with Ben about tracts he might be able to buy. After our return to Missouri he wrote several letters about property that was for sale on the reservation, but no purchase was ever made. Money was scarce, and the book was not the success he had hoped. It is probable that this lack of funds, together with other considerations, made buying land impossible. After these many years, I still like to return to Pine Ridge Reservation, for to me the land is as beautiful as in 1931.

After we returned home in the fall of 1931, Alice and I performed for local school affairs an Indian ceremony planned by our father. We used the drum Black Elk had played during the interviews, which my father had later obtained from Standing Bear, its owner. Accompanied by a very simple drumbeat, we sang a couple of songs I had learned from Leo Looks Twice and at the dances, recited parts of Black Elk's prayer, and told about the sacred hoop, the four quarters, the sky, and Mother Earth. Even though it was new to most of them, schoolchildren and townspeople seemed interested.

Because of the Missouri humidity, the drumhead would not stay taut for any length of time, and we placed it over a light bulb to tighten the skin so it could be played. Somehow the hot bulb touched the drum, burning a hole. Preserved in the museum at the John G. Neihardt Center in Bancroft, Nebraska, the drum still carries the leather patch my father used to repair it.

Shortly after our return from Manderson, Ben wrote to tell my father that a baby boy had been born, and that he and Ellen had named the child Jon-na-ha. We were all very happy about the new little Black Elk and appreciated their giving him a name that reflected the friendship they felt for "Jon Naha." Unfortunately the little fellow did not live long enough for us to get to know him.

The concept of the sacred hoop of the people, which had so impressed my father, did the same for Mother, and my parents wanted to create a garden based on the hoop. Perhaps it was the many formal gardens my mother had seen in Europe that prompted the idea, and the two soon worked out a plan for one to be built in our backyard. My father hired a man from the hill country to help, and I remember the problem he encountered when he tried to explain his plan to Art Combs. When he mentioned a garden, Art thought he understood: "Oh, a vegetable garden." "No," Daddy replied, "it will have flowers and bushes."

"A *flower* garden?"

"No, not a flower garden," Dad explained; "it will have a hedge around it and benches beside a pool."

Now Art Combs understood. "A *beauty* garden!" he exclaimed.

"Yes," Daddy replied, "a beauty garden."

And so the first sacred hoop prayer garden was born. It was enclosed by a large circle of privet hedge, and across the circle two roads were placed—the hard black road and the good red road. Where the two roads crossed was a small pool holding a fountain figure made by our mother, with the rising water representing the tree of life. It was a beautiful garden, and some years later I was married there in a ceremony that included concepts from Black Elk's vision. The garden in Branson was destroyed years ago, but another such garden has been built on the grounds of the Neihardt Center in Bancroft, where it is visited by people who also find its concept inspiring.

During the summer of 1934, when our father was writing his *Song of the Messiah,* Alice and I camped with him in a tent in a beautiful shady spot beside Wounded Knee Creek on Ben Black Elk's land near Manderson, South Dakota. What a happy summer we had! Sitting inside the tent or outside in the shade of a tree, Daddy wrote in the morning, and during the afternoons we had fun doing things with him.

Alice and I saw to the housekeeping chores of camping, keeping clothes and bedding clean and dry, and Daddy and I shared the cooking, often having freshly caught trout flopping in the pan at breakfast. Alice and I rose early and fished, many times still in our pajamas, using grasshoppers for bait. We had plenty of fresh fish that summer, and Ellen supplied us with vegetables from their garden. Fruit, which we especially liked, was scarce, and I remember how we laughed as we divided prunes, purchased at the Manderson trading post, among the three of us: "One for you, one for you, and one for me."

Dishes and utensils were kept clean and bright by washing them with sand in the creek or a nearby spring. We took baths in a part of Wounded Knee Creek where the bed was gravel and the stream flowed swiftly and commented that we were bathing in clean, fresh water at all times—*so* much better than a bathtub!

Black Elk was working in Colorado that summer, so we did not see him, but we had a fine time with Ben and Ellen and their family. Alice and I particularly remember their children Henry and Esther, though I am sure Grace and Olivia were there too. Henry was around most of the time, and I remember how he helped his father with the chores. Ben would call out "Hen-*ry!*" or "Son-*ny!*" and then in an imperious voice—perhaps for our benefit—tell Henry to do something, in Lakota of course. Then, as Henry set about the job, Ben would turn to us and grin. Just why he did that I do not know; perhaps it was to soften what to us seemed his unnecessarily harsh tone.

Not understanding Lakota, we did not know what Henry was told to do, but we did see the results: he would get on his horse, ride off like the wind, and carry out Ben's instructions with the cattle or horses. I don't know how old Henry was in 1934, but I well remember his prowess as a horseman.

Ben had given us permission to ride any of the horses in his large herd, and Alice and I took full advantage of his generosity. At home we had just one horse of our own, so having so many horses we could ride was exciting. The ponies ran free on the range, and catching them was a problem, but we soon found a way that worked for a while. We found we could catch horses by approaching them on hands and knees, for at first they didn't seem to realize we were people. When we got near a horse in this novel manner, we would throw a rope loosely over its neck. The horse, which had been roped before and knew it hurt to resist, stood still until we fastened the line about its head. But the horses soon caught on to our ruse, so we had to devise another means of catching them.

We had, of course, read about how the Indians used to ride with just a thong tied around the horse's lower jaw, so we tried that, using a rope. It worked, though not as well as a bridle. Most of the time we rode bareback, and the beautiful grasslands and bluffs were the backdrop for many a fine adventure.

We did enjoy it when Esther rode with us, and on one occasion we all saddled up, our father included, and helped Ben round up his herd of cattle. I don't know how much we *helped*, for the horses we rode knew more about herding cattle than we did. It was mostly a matter of staying on as the horse darted from side to side to keep the cattle in line, but it was a fine, dusty experience, and we learned why cowboys wear bandanas over their faces.

One day stands out in my memory. Alice and I rode alone up on the white, pine-studded bluffs across Wounded Knee Creek in sight of Ben's house. When we reached the top of the bluffs, we slid off our horses, and holding the reins, sat on the edge of the bluff looking down on the valley below, where our campsite lay hidden in the trees. We had a strange, mystical feeling as we sat high on those wonderful bluffs, with nothing at all around us. We talked of many things, Alice and I, but on this occasion she was thinking about the future she dreamed of, in which she hoped horses would play a part. "Why *can't* we raise horses?" Alice's face was earnest as she spoke. Knowing she meant this as a lifetime career, I responded, "Oh, Alice, I don't think that would work out." But my sister has made a career of breeding

American Saddlebreds, and she has trained more than one world champion. So much for the advice of an older sister.

We became especially fond of one of the horses we rode that summer. Barney was a chunky little bay gelding, and Ben wanted to give him to us. Because of the difficulty and no doubt the expense of getting the horse back to Missouri my dad could not accept the gift, but how nice it would have been to take Barney home with us.

During the 1934 summer my dad bought a steer, which our friends butchered and the women dried on racks made of small saplings fastened to poles that we helped set up near our camp. It was the old-time, proven way of preserving meat, and I was surprised that none of it spoiled, uncovered outdoors in the heat. We took the delicious dried *bapa* home to Missouri, where it unfortunately *did* spoil in the humid heat.

Unlike the first time we were there, it rained that summer, and one night, during a particularly heavy downpour complete with thunder and lightning, our tent flap was pulled open and Ben's sharp, wet face shone in the light of his lantern. "Don't you want to come up to the house?" he said. Warm and comfortable in our tent—and dry as well—we thanked Ben kindly but said we would stay where we were. Ben's thoughtful gesture remains in my memory, for he had walked nearly a mile in the torrential rain because he and Ellen were concerned about us.

One day a missionary or preacher came to call on my father. The two men sat on the grass under a tree for an hour or so, chatting and expressing in a friendly fashion their differing views. When the good man finally decided to go, my father accompanied him to the gate across the road from Ben's home. Returning to our campsite, Daddy chuckled as he told us how the preacher, who may have been worried about my father's spiritual welfare, had expressed that concern as they parted. This is how I remember those parting comments:

The preacher: "But don't you fear God?"

Neihardt's reply: "Fear God? No! God and I are good friends!"

The summer passed all too soon, as summers have a habit of doing, and we three were very sad when the time came to leave our friends and the spot where we had been so happy. I was returning to college in

Wayne, Nebraska, and to have more time for fun we decided we would stay an extra week on the reservation, and then my dad and Alice would drop me off at school on the way home. We did that, and I landed for my second year of college—at a strange school—with nothing to wear but breeches and boots! After a few embarrassing days I did receive some proper college clothes from home, and all was well.

The 1944 Interviews

The next time we saw Black Elk and his family was in 1944 when I went with my father for additional interviews with Black Elk and another old Sioux named Eagle Elk. This time I served as reporter, recording the conversations on a small typewriter balanced on my lap. My father was then employed as an information specialist at the Bureau of Indian Affairs in Chicago, working with his good friend John Collier, then director of the Bureau of Indian Affairs. Collier wanted material on the social history of the Sioux, and the literary result of these 1944 interviews is found in *When the Tree Flowered*. Although not so well known as *Black Elk Speaks,* this later book is equally authentic.

This time my father and I drove to the reservation in my automobile, and we did have great experiences together. Strangely, however, I do not recall as much detail about the 1944 interviews as about those conducted many years before. In 1931 what happened was all that was on my mind; in 1944 I was married, my husband had been sent overseas in the war, and I was planning to join the Waves myself.

I do remember how much Black Elk had changed since 1931: he was much older, of course, but I particularly noticed, and remarked about it to my father, that he looked much more Chinese than what we usually think of as Indian. His skin, formerly almost black, was now a golden tan, and his high cheekbones and the roundness of his face gave him an Oriental appearance. No doubt he was lighter because he was doing less outdoor work.

During our interviews with his father Ben again did the interpreting, and when I think back to those times I often see his earnest face, his penetrating eyes. Ben really cared, and it showed.

We did not live with the Black Elks in 1944. Since my father was employed by the BIA, we stayed at what was called "the club," a modest brick government building in Pine Ridge, and we ate our meals with the others there. Perhaps the food was not gourmet, but how we loved their fried pheasant!

For his talks with Eagle Elk my father used another interpreter, whom I do not recall; I remember only that it was not Ben. Eagle Elk was in his nineties and presented an impressive appearance. His long, flowing hair was white. His lean body was severely bent, so that his back was almost parallel to the ground, and he walked slowly with a cane, but his chiseled face and sparkling eyes revealed the handsome man he once had been. Through the interpreter, he joked about his aging and told us that when he was a young warrior he was tall and straight and very good to look at, and all the girls liked him. We did not doubt that.

Eagle Elk refused to live in a cabin like a white man, and our interviews were conducted in his tent home, which was near his daughter's house. The canvas wall tent was warmed by a sheet-metal stove, and my dad and I carried chunks of wood to keep it going through the cold days of late November and early December.

I was greatly touched the day my father bought the old man a gift, a pair of warm sheepskin slippers that he badly needed for he was often barefoot in the poorly heated tent. Taking the handsome new slippers out of the sack in which he had brought them from the trading post at Manderson, my father with considerable difficulty managed to work them onto Eagle Elk's bare feet, amid chuckles and smiles from the old warrior.

One day, as he neared the end of his life story, Eagle Elk told why he no longer had the leather quirt that had been so important to him in earlier years. "After my woman died," he told us, "I put the quirt down inside her dress. You see, I would not need it anymore!" Once again I felt how akin we were to our Indian relatives.

Eagle Elk's vision, which gave him his power as a warrior and his purpose as a man, ended with the voice of a high-flying eagle that cried out to him: "Hold fast! There is more!" That cry reechoed through his lifetime and gave him courage to persevere in difficult situations. For this reason the eagle was of special meaning to him, as was the eagle-bone whistle. After he had told us about its use and its great spiritual significance, one day he showed us such a whistle. That night something remarkable happened to my dad and me.

At the club we shared our quarters, sleeping in beds on opposite sides of the room. Sometime during the night Daddy suddenly awakened and sat bolt upright in bed, calling out to me: "Did you hear *that?*" "Yes, I did!" Indeed, the sound of an eagle-bone whistle had awakened us both, and I shall never forget its shrill, piercing tone there in the early-morning darkness.

What it meant and precisely who blew the whistle I shall leave to the reader to determine.

We Lose Black Elk, Ben, Neihardt, Leo, and Lucy

In addition to his interviews with Black Elk in 1944, my father saw his good friend more than once while employed by the Bureau of Indian Affairs. In 1945 they appeared together at the Victory Celebration in Pine Ridge, for which my father gave the main address. A photograph shows the two, both in rumpled suits, standing side by side, my father's arm around the holy man. A letter to my father from Black Elk received some time after the celebration informed him that "the Siouxs sure did appreciate what you said."

Black Elk died in 1950. A sign beside his grave in Manderson announces that it is the resting place of "Chief Black Elk," a title we never heard him use.

Although *Black Elk Speaks* had very little commercial success when it came out in 1932 and quickly went out of print, in nonetheless attracted widespread attention from persons who were intrigued by its authentic revelations of Lakota culture and spirituality. Among those who wrote to my father with particular enthusiasm was Joseph Epes Brown, and he requested that Neihardt help him meet the Lakota holy man. Because of Black Elk's previous reluctance to discuss his life or his experiences, my father replied that he doubted the old Lakota would see him but that perhaps he and Brown might meet and talk at length about Black Elk. Another communication repeated Brown's strong desire to know Black Elk personally and urged that my father do what he could to arrange a meeting.

I do not have a copy of the letter Neihardt then wrote to Black Elk, so I am not able to give its exact date. It was probably after my father and mother returned to their Branson home in 1946 after their stay in Chicago while my father worked at the Bureau of Indian Affairs. Whatever the date, I recall the incident well, for I typed my father's letter to his old friend. As I remember it, we were in his study when he dictated the letter to me.

In that letter my father told Black Elk that a young man named Joseph Epes Brown had written that he had been deeply moved by *Black Elk Speaks* and wanted to make the holy man's acquaintance. I remember the sense and almost the exact wording of that letter: Neihardt told Black Elk that he felt that Brown was a fine young man and that his interest in spiritual and religious matters was sincere. He went on to ask Black Elk to talk with him.

In his introduction to *The Sacred Pipe,* however, the author makes no mention of Neihardt's intervention on his behalf. The reader might get the impression that Brown was unaware of the complimentary letter of introduction Neihardt had written to Black Elk. If that is so it is regrettable, for not only does it reveal an unfortunate misunderstanding, it also omits events that may well figure in scholarly history. Because I remember the incident so clearly, and have more than once heard my father relate it substantially as I have recalled, it seems important that the Brown–Neihardt–Black Elk correspondence be recorded.

Ten years passed before we saw Ben again; it was in 1955 when he and Ellen came to Columbia, Missouri. Both were dressed—a first for us—in fine Sioux regalia. Ben had for some time been traveling all over the United States and Europe, telling about his father and explaining the concepts of Indian spirituality that had come to mean so much to him since he had learned of them through the 1931 and 1944 interviews. In spite of its lack of financial success, *Black Elk Speaks* had brought a new awareness of Sioux culture, and both father and son became known through it. Black Elk too had something of a career for several years, performing with the Duhamel Pageant in the Black Hills.

My family and I were very happy to see Ben and Ellen. They came to dinner at our home, which gave me a chance to return in small part the courtesies they had shown us more than twenty years before. Naturally we talked about that time of all times, our visit in 1931. Apropos of those talks, Ben remarked to my father that before he heard his father's story he was just a "dumb cowboy." To which my father replied, "Oh, Ben, we *both* learned."

During this visit in Columbia, my father and Ben had the opportunity to do something they had discussed before: Daddy recited his "Death of Crazy Horse" from *The Song of Indian Wars,* then Ben sang a death chant or memorial song. The event was videotaped at the University of Missouri as part of the course my father was then teaching.

Another videotape was made during the visit by Charles Sigsbee, television director at the University of Missouri. In that tape Neihardt told how he happened to meet Black Elk, described the book as "the complete story of the developing life of a holy man from his youth to his old age," and introduced Ben and his wife, Ellen. With proper modesty, Ellen Black Elk sat with downcast eyes during the interview and did not speak, but Ben spoke at length, sang, and showed how the sacred pipe should be offered in prayer. A transcription of this videotape appears in the appendix of this book.

After their 1955 visit I did not see Ben and Ellen again, nor perhaps did my father, although he corresponded regularly with Ben and helped him from time to time when, in later years, Ben was no longer working, was not well, and lacked financial resources. Ellen died in 1970, followed by Ben in March 1973. Ben was given a large, well-publicized funeral at which his grandsons were pallbearers. My father, then in his ninety-third year, was at my home taping recitations and interviews for a United Artists album to be called "Flaming Rainbow" and was unable to attend the funeral service.

In August John Neihardt returned from Lincoln, Nebraska, to our home near Columbia, Missouri, to spend what we hoped would be some remaining years. On November 3, 1973, family members and some special friends were gathered at his bedside. Looking directly at me, my father did not speak, but he tapped the middle finger of his right hand several times on his chest. Then, with something like a *whoosh* we felt his great spirit leave. He had embarked on the great adventure.

After the funeral service Alice and I, accompanied by Bob Dyer, a young University of Missouri teacher who was a special friend of my father's, were flown to the nearby Missouri River by the owner of a local private airport. As her twin-engine plane circled low over a broad bend in the Missouri, Alice and I opened the windows and emptied containers holding the ashes of our father and of our mother, who had died in 1958, permitting their remains to mingle as they fell into the river that had figured so strongly in our father's writings. Alice had brought a copy of his *Lyric and Dramatic Poems,* and we held it together, reading silently the lyric "When I Have Gone Weird Ways." The overwhelming emotion of the moment prevented my reciting the poem aloud as we had planned. Thus was our parents' expressed wish carried out.

A few weeks later came the Thanksgiving holiday, and we decided to repeat the family gathering that had been such a happy annual affair when our parents were living. The whole Neihardt clan living near Columbia were to gather at my hilltop farm home, and we made the traditional preparations.

Just about midday my son Robin and I were in the front yard awaiting the arrival of my sisters, Enid and Alice, and their families. "Look, Mother, there's an *eagle!*" Robin pointed eagerly to the sky, and I saw it too. A big bald eagle was flying toward us from the south, and as we watched, it descended, very low and directly over our house, made a circle, flew away, then returned and flew over the house once more— only a few feet above the roof. Then it left and quickly disappeared to the south where it had come from.

Just as the eagle was going over the house for the second time, Alice and her daughter Lynn drove up. Looking where we excitedly pointed, Lynn said: "I've never seen an eagle before in my whole life!" Indeed, eagles were seldom found in that area. As I watched the big bird disappear in the distance, I thought of the eagle feathers on the daybreak star ornament and on the sacred pipe, and I wondered about Black Elk.

All these years I had been working as a lawyer and living with my three children on a farm near Columbia. Though I had been unable to go back to South Dakota to see our Lakota friends, Leo and Lucy and the others were often in my mind. Then one day in 1974 I received a letter from Lucy, beginning "Dear Niece Hilda." I was happy to receive the letter, but when I read the news it contained, I pounded in angry sorrow on the kitchen counter. Leo had died, Lucy said, and she thought I would want to hear about it. She added that he had spoken often of the times we went riding together. Oh, those wonderful, bright times in that beautiful land! They would never happen again.

Lucy's letter brought us together again after many years, and she visited me on the farm. A friend of mine, then dean of faculty at Stephens College in Columbia, had the remarkable insight to realize that Lucy Black Elk Looks Twice, who had lived all her life on Pine Ridge Reservation, would have something to tell the girls at that elite college. Dr. Littleton invited Lucy to speak at Stephens, and speak she did! Sitting in a large chair in one of the college's comfortable lounges, with young women from many parts of the country listening, Lucy spoke with the natural dignity I have found is typical of the Lakotas.

Lucy told about her life on the reservation, about her father, and about her husband and his death. Then she said something so striking that I seem to remember her exact words: "When my old man died," Lucy remarked, "my religion [she had been a lifelong member of a white church] *did not help me any*. When I told my friends this, they said, 'Why don't you read the book about your father?' And so, for the first time, I did read *Black Elk Speaks*."

Before Lucy could continue, a student raised her hand and asked, "And what did reading the book do for you?" "It changed my life!" was Lucy's response.

The college newspaper *Stephens Life,* reported the event in its April 7, 1977, edition, and I quote part of that article: "Lucy Looks Twice never knew about her father's spiritual visions; he never told her. But Looks Twice, the daughter of Black Elk, a Sioux holy man, heard of his visions and believed in them as Black Elk recalled them to the late John G. Neihardt, UMC professor."

During the days Lucy visited me, I took her to see Alice, who lives in our parents' home in Columbia, Skyrim. Taking Lucy to her stables, Alice enthusiastically showed her American saddlebreds—foals, stallions, broodmares, and mature, trained performers. Lucy was deeply impressed and described them fittingly: "They are like spirit horses!"

Lucy, of course, wanted to see Enid, so we went to her home for a visit with Enid and her husband, the journalist Oliver Fink. Enid and Lucy talked at length about "old times" and the good memories both had of the 1931 visit. Enid confided to me later that Lucy had told her, "You know, Enid, when you were with us in 1931, I thought you were a little fast with our warriors. But I don't think so anymore."

During the time she spent at my home, Lucy told me a few old stories, some of which I tape-recorded. We made plans for the public appearances we hoped to make in the future, at which Lucy would tell stories or sing Lakota songs and I would recite Neihardt's poetry. How excited we were about this idea!

Unfortunately, except for one time, Lucy and I were not able to carry out our plans. At the annual Neihardt Day in Bancroft, Nebraska, in August 1977, we recited Black Elk's Prayer—first Lucy spoke in Lakota, then I gave it in English, with Lucy chanting in the background. Tom Allan, longtime friend of my father's and well-known staff writer for the Omaha *World-Herald,* interpreted what Lucy and I did at the Neihardt Center:

Daughters Join Hands In Bridging Eternity
Two daughters, Morning Star and Lucy Looks Twice, bridged a gap in eternity Sunday.

They stood together, in bright sunshine, beside the Sioux Prayer Garden and joined in offering Black Elk's Prayer, made famous by their fathers.

We were all very sad when Lucy died in 1978. Her funeral service combined Catholic and Lakota traditions. After the service and the giveaway that followed, while we visited at the home of Esther and Aaron De Sersa Sr., Esther told me that Lucy had often spoken about our plans to perform together. It was good to know that Lucy felt as I did. I would miss her, for she was truly her father's daughter.

While Lucy was in Columbia a warm and trusting closeness developed between us, and Lucy told me about the deaths of her father and Ben. She said that in 1950 Black Elk was very ill, and members of the family gathered around him in his Manderson home. The old man did not live long, but before he passed away, Lucy revealed, Black Elk told them, "The only thing I really believe is the pipe religion." The term "pipe religion" was one I had never heard before, but Lucy's meaning was clear.

Then Lucy told me how Ben had died on the way to the hospital in Rapid City. While still at home, Lucy said, her half-brother also expressed to her and others in the family his true beliefs: "He told us the same thing," Lucy said, and I knew what she meant.

Just why Lucy revealed those things to me I did not know, nor did I wonder about it at the time. Certainly what she said was not in response to any inquiry from me. I have recently learned that in 1973 or thereabouts Lucy had talked to a writer about Black Elk's work as a Catholic catechist, and a book has now appeared based on those communications.

Lucy didn't mention to me that she had ever spoken to anyone about her father's life. Now, having learned about her conversations with the author, and because Lucy placed noticeable emphasis on what she told me, I think that the statements she had made were probably disturbing to her after she had finally—so late in life—read *Black Elk Speaks*. It is apparent that becoming aware of her native beliefs from that book held great meaning for her; in fact, as she had told her audience at Stephens College, it changed her life. During her last years, Lucy carried her own sacred pipe with her: she had become a pipe carrier.

Because she knew it would be important to me, I believe she felt I should know what her father had revealed to his family before he died, and what Ben had told them. I am happy that Lucy wanted me to know. I trust in what she told me: Isn't it always important that the truth be known?

And Now Today

Now I look back once more to 1930, and to what Black Elk expressed to a man he had just met: "I feel in this man beside me a great desire to know the things of the other world. He has been *sent* to learn what I will teach him, and he must come back in the spring when the grass is so high." Later he told Neihardt, "If the vision was true and mighty then, it is true and mighty yet, and you were sent to save it."

As I think about that remarkable happening and about the teachings of Black Elk that Neihardt incorporated into *Black Elk Speaks,* one thought stands out above all others in my mind: how faithfully the poet *did* keep his promise to the holy man. After they met in 1930, Neihardt wrote to Black Elk that he would listen to what he planned to teach him and would put those teachings into "a beautiful and true book." He implicitly promised, then and during the interviews, that he would carry out Black Elk's expressed wish: he would save the vision for those it was meant for; it would be saved *for all people*.

Throughout his life, John Neihardt made his living to a great extent by teaching and lecturing, and I dare say that during the forty years or so he carried on after he became acquainted with the holy man, *never* did he speak to an audience without telling them something about "my good friend Black Elk." In classes, on college platforms, and more than once in churches, my father told audiences about Black Elk, about the sacred hoop and the great vision, and he recited a shortened version of Black Elk's Prayer as he had set it in English words:

Grandfather, Great Mysterious One, you have been
   always, and before you nothing has been.

There is nothing to pray to but you.

The star nations all over the universe are yours, and
  yours are the grasses of the earth.

Day in, day out, you are the life of things.

You are older than all need, older than all pain and
  prayer.

Grandfather, all over the world the faces of living
  ones are alike.

In tenderness they have come up out
  of the ground. Look upon your children with children
  in their arms, that they may face the winds and walk
  the Good Road to the Day of Quiet.

Teach me to walk the soft earth, a relative to all that
  live.

Sweeten my heart, and fill me with light. Give
  me the strength to understand and the eyes to see.

Help me, for without you, I am nothing.

Hetchetu aloh!

Yes, the years go, but memories of the times we spent with Black
Elk and his family do not dim.

I live beside the Missouri River in Nebraska in a house I call Daybreak, remembering the name Black Elk gave me. As the sun rises over
my great river, often I watch with wonder and amazement the beauty
of the breaking day, and more and more I feel that I *am* Daybreak Star
Woman. I think often of the sacred hoop, which Black Elk told us is
large enough to hold all living things with legs or wings or roots, and
within which we should live together, as Ben said it, like "relateeves."

I like to walk, alone or with my family or friends, along a small road
that crosses the fields west of my home. As I stroll through the broad
green, brown, or snow-whitened Nebraska land under the arching,
deep-blue prairie sky whose horizon stretches in a broad circle around
me, Black Elk's description of the sacred hoop comes alive. Again I see
in my thoughts the sacred tree that stands where the good red road of
spiritual understanding crosses the hard black road of worldly diffi-

culties. I realize why that crossing place is holy and why it takes strength to understand.

My heart rises as I gaze about me, and my being is in tune with the words Black Elk spoke as we sat cross-legged on the grass of Standing Bear's land more than sixty years ago:

You can just look around you and see that it is so!

Appendix
Remembering Black Elk

This is a transcription of a videotaped conversation between Ben Black Elk and John Neihardt that took place in 1955 in the library-study at Neihardt's home in Columbia, Missouri. Ellen Black Elk, Ben's wife, was also present, though she did not speak. Both Ben and Ellen were dressed in traditional Sioux clothing, and Ben's face was painted. The filming was done by Charles Sigsbee of the University of Missouri television staff. Although the videotape was made in 1955, I did not see a copy of it until after the manuscript for this book was finished.

NEIHARDT: My friends, I have a book in my library that I'd like to tell you about. It's one of my books. [Neihardt takes a book from the shelf.] It's called *Black Elk Speaks,* and it tells the complete story of the developing life of a holy man from his youth to his old age.

His name, the holy man's name, is Black Elk. He has been dead now five years, but his fame lives after him. He's known all over the United States among anthropologists and psychologists and people who are interested in the American Indians, and he is also known in Europe. It has recently appeared in a German edition, and it interested people over there a great deal.

Now I want to tell you how I happened to do this book and what the meaning of the book is. Later on I'll have a nice surprise for you.

It was during the time when I was working on the fifth narrative of my heroic cycle of the West, which is called *A Cycle of the West.* This fifth narrative is entitled *The Song of the Messiah,* and it deals with what white men called "the Messiah craze," which took place among all the

Indians in the United States from the middle eighties on to about December 29, 1890. It ended with the slaughter at Wounded Knee on December 29, 1890.

Now, I had all the records on this movement—on the Messiah movement. I knew the records, and I had talked to a number of old Sioux who had been associated with it somewhat. I went to Pine Ridge Reservation to see Mr. Courtwright, the agent at the time, who was a fan of mine and knew my work well, and I told him what I wanted. There were a number of old Sioux there—longhairs, you know, who spoke no English. And he conferred with them, and they told him that about twenty miles over east there was an old man by the name of Ehaka Sapa, Black Elk, and that he was a kind of a preacher. What they really meant to say was that he was a *wichasha wakan,* that he was a holy man. That's perhaps what they said. And they said he had been in this movement and that he had had a vision from which they had developed the idea of the holy shirt which was used in the Messiah movement.

Well, we went over to see Black Elk. He lived over four miles from a log store that they called Manderson. He lived out in the barren hills in a one-room log cabin, and I had to have an interpreter, so I got a Sioux, a young Sioux by the name of Flying Hawk, to go over there with me. I told Flying Hawk what I wanted, and he said, "I'm afraid the old man won't talk to you." And I said, "How's that? I've known Indians for many years. They always talk to me." And he said, "Well, there is something peculiar about this old man. About two weeks ago there was a lady came up here who wanted to write an article on Crazy Horse."

Now Black Elk was second cousin to the great chief Crazy Horse, and she wanted to write an article on him. "Well," he said, "I took her over there and the old man, who was nearly blind for many years, he squinted at her, and finally he said, 'I can see that you are a nice looking woman, and I can feel that you are good, but I do not care to talk to you about these things.' And that's all she got."

Well, I thought maybe the old man was peculiar, but I said, "We'll go and see." And so we went over there. And when we arrived, Black Elk had been sitting under a pine shade out in front of his—oh, some distance from his little one-room log cabin—and we went there at noon. Now, we didn't get away until after sunset, and we'd been talking all the time.

When we left, Flying Hawk said, "Well, that was funny." And I said, "What was funny, Flying Hawk?" And he said, "Well, it seemed to me," he said, "that the old man was expecting you." And my son said, "You know, I had the same feeling." Well at the time I didn't—I hardly believed it—but later I came to believe it.

I sat down with him and we passed cigarettes around. There were several old men present who saw us coming and came over to see what was going to happen. I passed cigarettes around and I said to Black Elk, "I have heard of you, and I've come over to have a little talk." And he said, "Ah-h-h."

We sat there and we smoked, and he was looking at the ground. And finally he looked up and he said to Flying Hawk, "As I sit here, I can feel in this man beside me a strong desire to know the things of the other world." He meant the spirit world. "He has been sent here to learn what I know, and I will teach him."

Then he went into one of his silences again and was staring at the ground. And then he said something to his little grandson who was sitting there, and the little boy ran up on the hill to the log cabin and came back with this sacred ornament. [Neihardt removes ornament from around his neck and holds it out in front of him.] He held it up and he said, "Here you see the morning star. Who sees the morning star shall see more, for he shall be wise."

After that we talked. I knew, of course, the history of the Sioux well from records and from, of course, talks with old men. And I tried to engage him in conversation on old battles and the old hunts, and the old way of life. And he was a very polite man and he would reply in a polite way, but he wasn't interested in that. What he was interested in was his great vision that he had had when he was nine years old.

It was along about sunset when he said to me, "You have been sent here to learn what I know. This vision that I had is beautiful, and it is true, and it was given to me for men. And soon I shall be under the grass and it will be lost, and you must save it. You must come back so that I can teach you."

And I said, "When do you want me, Black Elk? I'll come back." And he said, "In the spring when the grass is this high." [Neihardt indicates with his hands a height of about four inches.] That would be in about May 1931. And I did go back.

But during that winter I arranged with his son Black Elk—he corresponded for the old man—for the meeting that we were to have in May. We went up there with my daughter Enid, who was my secretary at the time and very fast in stenography. She was to take down all the conversations.

So we went there, and they had everything arranged for a big meeting. We talked for about five weeks, beginning often in the early morning and talking sometimes up to ten or eleven o'clock at night. And the old man in that time told his great vision for the first time to the world, and it is the first time that a holy man's vision was ever given to the world. It is one of the most profoundly beautiful things in religious literature—it has been agreed that that is true. It took him seventeen days to tell his vision.

Now, I could not have gotten this without the cooperation of my friend Black Elk, Ben Black Elk, who is the son of Black Elk. The old man would not allow anyone to interpret for me but his son, because he said that others would not say, tell, what he said, and his son Ben would. So Ben interpreted for me and was the go-between between Black Elk and myself.

And here is my old friend and spiritual brother, Benjamin Black Elk, son of the great holy man Black Elk. He feels as I do that we have a sacred obligation to carry on for the old man and to spread abroad the news of his beautiful and profoundly true teaching. Ben has been doing that ever since, and I have, as much as I could.

We also have with us Mrs. . . . Mrs. Ellen Black Elk. I have a special feeling for Mrs. Black Elk. I lived at her house quite a long while, and I visited at their home, and she was always such a charming, sweet hostess. And I wish I could have one of her good meals again! I think I'll have to go back for that. Ben, you and I have had a great privilege, haven't we?

BEN: That's right.

NEIHARDT: You had the greater privilege, because you are the real son of Black Elk. But I feel that I am the spiritual son of Black Elk, and you and I are brothers.

BEN: You are right on that. But I always feel that you, you were the one that brought it out. I am the son, but still you made it possible to . . . to reach a lot of people.

NEIHARDT: Ben, I couldn't have gotten it through any other man, because the old man wouldn't let anybody else talk, and you understood about him.

BEN: I understood, yes, that's right.

NEIHARDT: Yes, that's exactly it. Ben, do you remember the time when we went up to Harney Peak with the old man?

BEN: Yes, I do.

NEIHARDT: Remember he was taken to the center of the world in his vision?

BEN: That's right.

NEIHARDT: And do you remember what he saw there in his vision?

BEN: That's right. I always remember that while we was going up—he was old, you know—and he wanted to go up, and he was in a rush. I asked him to sit down and said, "Why, father, are you in a rush?" And he said, "Well, son, you probably know what I told you about my vision, and you probably know now about the tree—the tree of life." And he said, "That's where I saw the whole works. Everybody was in unity under the Great Spirit."

NEIHARDT: Under the great tree, under the great tree of life.

BEN: Now, he said, "There's going to be something happen up there *today*. See, that tree has withered; it's all withered. But if there is a little root that is living, something is going to happen. And if I and my vision is true," he said, "the thunder beings will answer my prayers."

NEIHARDT: There should be a little thunder and a little rain.

BEN: A little thunder and a little rain, yes.

NEIHARDT: Yes.

BEN: So as we went up, he undressed and stood the same place where he stood . . .

NEIHARDT: . . . in his vision.

BEN: Yes. And then he started to send his voice to the Great Spirit as he prayed. You know the words to that prayer.

NEIHARDT: I know the prayer, yes.

BEN: And he asked the Great Spirit if there was a little life in that tree, to water it to make it alive. And he who so wanted a vision given, to give to the world, that he would believe himself to the Great Spirit. And then you know he cried, and I cried with him.

NEIHARDT: We all did. Tears running down his cheeks, yes.

BEN: Then when he got through praying, you know the thunders . . .

NEIHARDT: The clouds came . . .

BEN: . . . the clouds came. It thundered and it rained.

NEIHARDT: It rained about five minutes. And we could see seventy-five miles everyplace—and it was *clear*.

BEN: It was clear . . .

You know, that place there, Black Hills are a sacred place to the Sioux Nation even today, although we lost it away, even yet so today.

NEIHARDT: That's right, that's right. Ben, I remember how amazed you and I used to be when the old man would say some of these strangely beautiful, profound things. I'd say to you, "Ben, *did he say that?*" And you'd say, "Yes, he said just that."

BEN: That's right. That's right. Exactly. That's what he said.

NEIHARDT: We couldn't believe our ears, you know. It was so wonderful. And I remember once, you and I were out riding together, out in the hills, and you said to me, "Isn't it wonderful?" And I said, "What?" And you said, "What the old man is saying. I always knew he had something, but I never knew what it was. It's wonderful."

And I remember one really remarkable thing that he said. We can't go into the vision; it takes too long. But once we were out on Pepper Creek. Remember, he was telling you why he called me Flaming Rainbow?

BEN: Oh, yes, I do remember.

NEIHARDT: You tell them then.

BEN: Well, you know, I always remember that. We knew that you are a poet, but we have no word that translates for poet, so he called you a word sender. And he said, "A word sender. And it's just like a garden, a flower garden. And it's just like rain on a flower garden. And that the words, as you go past, why, it leaves some of it and then leaves it green. And then when it is gone, at the end when you're gone," he said, "your words will be memories, and it will be always a long time in the west—as a flaming rainbow."

NEIHARDT: That's right. Exactly. It was one of the most beautiful things I'd ever heard, but it was strange. Well, now, Ben, you're a good singer, and there's a beautiful prayer that the old man taught me and I have spread it all over the United States.

BEN: Oh, yes. Uh-huh.

NEIHARDT: And you know the prayer as well as I do. It's a shorter form of one of his long prayers. They are the most beautiful things, I think, in religious literature. I don't know anything more beautiful than those prayers, and they have meaning. You remember that one? I wish you—you'll have to sing a song first, won't you?

BEN: Sure. You know the words to this song all right. I'm sure you know it. It's in *Black Elk Speaks*. The words are: "I'm sending a voice; I'm sending a voice. O Great Spirit, hear me."

[Ben sings a song in Lakota, using his drum, then offers the pipe to the four quarters, the sky, and the earth and prays, "Tunkashila. . . . "]

Index